TREASURES OF LORD'S

The MCC
CRICKET
LIBRARY

TREASURES OF LORD'S

WILLOW BOOKS
Collins
8 Grafton Street, London W1
1989

Willow Books
William Collins Sons & Co. Ltd
London · Glasgow · Sydney · Auckland
Toronto · Johannesburg

First published 1989
© MCC and Tim Rice 1989

BRITISH LIBRARY CATALOGUING IN PUBLICATION DATA
Rice, Tim
Treasures of Lord's.
1. Cricket. Memorabilia
I. Title
796.35'8

ISBN 0-00-218307-2

Set in Sabon by
Rowland Phototypesetting Ltd
Bury St Edmunds, Suffolk
Originated, printed and bound in Singapore by
C. S. Graphics Pte Ltd

Contents

List of Illustrations

Part One: Lord and Lord's

Part Five: Curiouser and Curiouser

II

Foreword

I am delighted, as the current President of the Marylebone Cricket Club, to write an introduction to this handsomely illustrated book, the *Treasures of Lord's*, which is the first of a highly selective series of cricket books, in which the intention is to make use of (although not exclusively) MCC's magnificent library, picture and archive material.

MCC no longer controls the first-class game but, in running and developing Lord's Cricket Ground, having a missionary role towards the amateur game and the coaching of youth generally, formulating the Laws of the game and administering the International Cricket Conference, it is still very much the Headquarters of Cricket and, to some extent, its guardian and conscience as well. As such, maintaining the historical records and artefacts of the game, of which Lord's has a unique collection, is a very important part of MCC's responsibilities; and it is only right that some of these treasures should now be seen by a wider public.

The first volume will bring to readers more than a hundred of the Club's finest possessions, and this will be followed first by a historical record of the oldest first-class fixture held at Lord's – Oxford versus Cambridge – and then by three further volumes covering cricket at Lord's, or involving MCC, as seen through the eyes of the cartoonist and caricaturist, the artist and the photographer. Together these will provide a marvellous personal library and a very comprehensive record of the history of the game. I commend this volume and those which are to follow it to all lovers of cricket.

Field Marshal the Rt Hon. The Lord Bramall
President MCC
October 1988

Introduction

The third Lord's Cricket Ground, in St John's Wood, north London, home of the Marylebone Cricket Club since 1814, is a modest arena compared with many of the world's great sporting centres, and even compared with several other cricket grounds. Only 27,000 people (at a push) are officially allowed into the ground at any one time, although this figure has certainly been exceeded on occasion. Its facilities, as far as the paying member of the public is concerned, are not obviously impressive – Lord's retains the air of a club more than that of a stadium, which even the marvellous and exotic New Mound Stand (completed 1987) and the introduction in 1988 of an electronic scoreboard have done nothing to dispel.

But of course Lord's is so much more than the sum of its parts, even including the most impressive parts such as the magnificent Pavilion, completed in 1890. It is the premier home of cricket, a monument to the game's history and traditions, the one place where every cricketer wants to play. But Lord's is still a club as much as it is an international cricket ground. Even during the noisiest of games a member is able to wander around some of the remoter parts of the Pavilion and attached buildings and avail himself of many of the privileges of most long-established London clubs – a quiet snooze in front of the television, a drink in a convivial bar, a game of squash or of real tennis, or a browse in the library or reading room – and on top of that he can even watch cricket. Or he can admire the club's art collection.

Within the ground is housed the MCC's outstanding collection of pictures and the large number of items of cricketing memorabilia which have accumulated at Lord's over the years. Much of this is on show to the public in the Memorial Gallery behind the Pavilion. Many other items, primarily pictures, are displayed in the Pavilion itself, and these cannot be seen except on organized tours on non-match days by anyone other than the 18,000 members of the MCC. The majority of the best-known and most valuable paintings hang in the Long Room, the appropriately named room on the ground floor overlooking the playing area through which every cricketer playing at Lord's has to walk on his way to and from the action, and in which a large body of members is always stationed during every important game.

The Lord's collection was started in 1864 by Sir Spencer Ponsonby-Fane (see page 35). The club had been in existence for the best part of a century, at its final resting-place for half a century, and yet owned just two pictures. Ponsonby-Fane set out to establish the basis of a cricket collection that would not only be of artistic but also of historical importance – the success of his venture is reflected in this book. Ponsonby-Fane, who was Treasurer of the MCC from 1879 until his death in 1915 aged ninety-one, pursued his labour of love with un-flagging energy, watching out for cricketing pictures, portraits and prints in the auction rooms or as they appeared in dealers' showrooms, persuading friends and members to donate and also commissioning works on MCC's behalf.

So dramatically did the collection grow that there was soon not enough room for all of it. Many a cricketer, by no means all well known, bequeathed souvenirs of his playing days most generously to the MCC, who were however only able to afford permanent display to the most unusual or the most important. The shelf-life of many fascinating pieces of cricketing history was embarrassingly short or even non-existent; much of Sir Spencer's vision was gathering dust in the basement.

Consequently, a proposal of the MCC Arts and Library Sub-Committee under Mr T. M. B. Sissons that many of these lost items should be offered for sale at auction was approved by the Committee, and over eight hundred lots came under Christie's hammer in 1987. The sale was an enormous success; many cricket memorabilia auctions in the previous decade had demonstrated the enormous public interest in things cricketing, and the MCC received in all £290,000. A total of 845 works of art, including bats, balls, clothing, handkerchiefs, portraits, cartoons and prints, changed hands, moving to walls where they will be seen, one assumes, regularly by at least one admirer more than they had been while languishing at Lord's. Let it be noted here that every effort was made to contact surviving relatives of donors of pictures that went into the sale; the Committee would not have sanctioned sale had it been felt that this would have caused offence.

Besides giving a new lease of life to forgotten or duplicate gems, the MCC was now able to establish a fund with the proceeds of the sale to restore and improve the main collection. A century and a score of highlights of this collection is displayed within this book. A century and a score more could have been included had space permitted – but the brief of this book is not a history of cricket or even of its headquarters, although many strands of cricket's past are caught up in the story behind each and every item. From emu's egg and boomerang to Francis Hayman's renowned eighteenth-century portrayal of cricket in Mary-le-Bone Fields, from huge Lordscapes to a tiny stuffed sparrow, from Nyren to Cowdrey, from Hambledon to the Valley of Peace in Christchurch, New Zealand, the immortal appeal of the summer game shines out – as it did in Sir Spencer Ponsonby-Fane's time and as it will a century hence.

PART ONE

Lord and Lord's

In 1787 the Marylebone Cricket Club was formed by members of the White Conduit Club. In the same year Thomas Lord's ground on the site of Dorset Square staged its first match – Middlesex *v* Essex. The MCC itself did not grace Lord's ground until the following summer.

The founder of Lord's was born in 1755 in Thirsk, Yorkshire into a wealthy Catholic landowning family. His father, William, supported the Jacobite rising of 1745 and as a result of his involvement with this doomed enterprise had his land confiscated. The family eventually moved to Diss in Norfolk where Thomas was educated and first played cricket. In London as a young man he pursued both his interest in the game and a career in wine.

His cricket career was a modest one. He played occasionally for Middlesex and later for Epsom in first-class matches as a right-hand slow underarm bowler and a lower-order batsman. It is of course his skill in the property business that ensured his name sporting immortality. He became associated with the White Conduit Club, which has been described as 'the acorn from which sprang the gigantic oak known as the MCC', where he bowled to the Earl of Winchilsea and his friends in practice. The Earl and his friends offered financial support to Lord to create a private cricket ground. Lord seized this opportunity of patronage and secured a position in Dorset Square, about as far south of the Marylebone Road as the present ground is north, in May 1787. The Middlesex/Essex encounter started on 31 May, and Middlesex (Lord was not playing) won by 93 runs.

Lord's Dorset Square ground soon became established as London's principal cricket venue, and indeed played host to a variety of other sporting and social functions. Regiments paraded, pigeons were shot and internationally celebrated balloonists ascended into the clouds from a standing start on Lord's turf. Hopping races were also staged (a John Bentley won 29 of them). The MCC flourished, and in 1805 Eton and Harrow played the first of their series of matches that continues at Lord's to this day. The first Gentlemen *v* Players fixture took place there in 1806.

But the rapid expansion of London threatened the continued existence of Dorset Square as a pleasure resort. Its value as a building site was of greater interest to the freeholders, the Portman Estate, than its value as a recreational centre. They consequently proposed to raise Lord's rent considerably. Fortunately, Lord had anticipated the crisis some two years beforehand and even as the MCC met in the Pavilion for its last Anniversary Dinner in Dorset Square on 8 May 1810, he had already rented two fields on the St John's Wood Estate for an eighty-year term. He transferred much of the Dorset Square turf to his new ground, presumably to give his patrons the feeling that little had changed, but the MCC members in particular felt otherwise. They played no matches at Lord's in either 1811 or 1812 and only three in 1813. Worse, the Anniversary Dinner did not take place during Lord's tenure of his second ground. The place was deemed to lack atmosphere and prestige. Many members resigned and the very existence of the club was threatened. The final blow to Lord's attempt to establish himself on the Brick and Great Fields came in 1812 when Parliament announced plans to cut the Regent Canal through the middle of his ground.

Although the *Laws of Cricket* had at that time been established for a mere 68 years, Lord chose to move to a third ground rather than attempt to persuade the MCC to alter the structure of the game to incorporate a canal. He was fortunate that the Eyre family, whose fields he was now forced to vacate, were willing to grant him another plot within half a mile. In June 1813, or thereabouts, Lord took possession of his third ground and shifted his hallowed turf once more, purchasing a lease with nearly eighty years unexpired.

It took some time for Lord to bring his new HQ up to the standard of that of Dorset Square. Among his problems were water (again – this time in the form of two ponds) and an accidental explosion in the Tavern public house which formed part of Lord's leasehold. None the less he soon won back the confidence of the MCC, who played the first recorded match on the new site, against Hertfordshire, on 22 June 1814. The MCC won by an innings, and have made their headquarters at Lord's ever since.

In 1825 Lord, now aged seventy, obtained planning permission to build houses on his ground, but was persuaded instead (as perhaps he hoped he would be) to sell his interest in Lord's to William Ward for £5000. He and his wife continued to live close by the ground, in St John's Wood Road. Mrs Lord died in August 1828, aged seventy-four, and was buried in St John's Wood churchyard. Thomas Lord retired to West Meon in Hampshire, where he died on 13 January 1832, aged seventy-six. His simple gravestone in West Meon reads:

Sacred to the memory of Thomas Lord
Late of St John's Wood Road, Marylebone
who departed this life the 13th of January 1832
aged 76 years
Founder of Lord's Cricket Ground 1787

The portrait that hangs in the Long Room was at one time attributed to the English genre landscape and animal painter George Morland (1763–1804). It was presented to the MCC by Miss Florence Lord in 1931. If truly a Morland, it would have to have been painted before 1799, as the final years of the artist's life were a sad saga of dissipation, debt and ill health. In the portrait Lord looks a decade too old for Morland's easel. Lord in his prime, well-proportioned and robustly handsome, was five feet nine inches tall and weighed in at twelve stone.

———— I ————

LORD, Thomas
(1755–1832)
The founder of Lord's Cricket Ground
Oil on canvas 37″ × 32″
Artist unknown, formerly attributed to
George Morland (1763–1804)

This punch bowl, made in Jingdezhen, is the only piece of Chinese export porcelain which portrays cricket. On the outside of the bowl is a reproduction of Hayman's Mary-le-Bone Fields painting (see pages 61 and 62) probably known to the Chinese artist through the popular print after the painting. A Man-o'-War flying the Union Flag of pre-1801 appears on the inside of the bowl. The name 'Thirks' on the poop may have been intended to read 'Thirsk', the birthplace of Thomas Lord, which suggests that he himself may have commissioned this remarkable piece.

2

Punch bowl
Chinese porcelain; 6″ high, diameter at top 14″
c. 1786

Thomas and Amelia Lord. The
Lords had one son, Thomas, born
in 1794. He married Maria Harper
and had five children. Thomas Jr
died in 1875.

--- 3 ---
LORD, Thomas and Amelia
Silhouettes, *c.* 1820
Given to Lord's by Walter Townsend
in 1897
Artist unknown

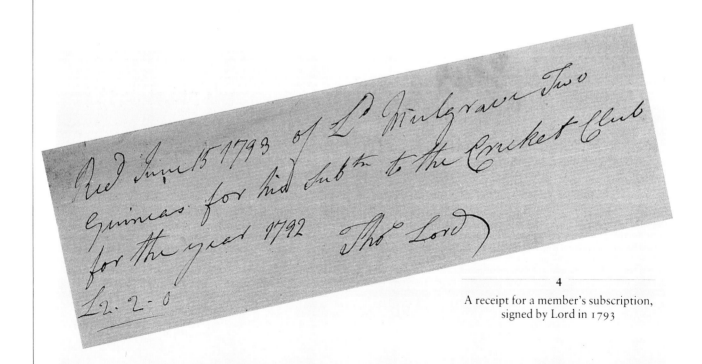

--- 4 ---
A receipt for a member's subscription,
signed by Lord in 1793

2nd Innings   Harrow

Ld Ipswich	0222111.3221	run	21
Farren	111	c. Bradley	3
Lloyd	0	b. Carter	0
Boulton	0	b. Heaton	0
Brockman	10	b. Heaton	10
Shakespear	5	run out	5
Dixon	6	st. Heaton	6
Erskine	0	b. Heaton	0
Ld Byron	2	b. Carter	2
Stanley	7	c. Canning	7
Asheton	0	not out	0
		Byes	3
			65

Byes — 111

The Harrow were beat in one Innings by 12 Notches easy

Hurra

Exeunt Omnes

—— 5 ——

Eton *v* Harrow Scorebook 1805

We have played the Eton and were most confoundedly beat; however it was some comfort to me that I got eleven notches in the first innings and seven in the second, which was more than any of our side, except Brockman and Ipswich, could contrive to hit. After the match we dined together, and were extremely friendly; not a single discordant word was uttered by either party. To be sure, we were most of us rather drunk, and went home together to the Haymarket, where we kicked up a row . . . How I got home after the play, God knows.

Byron's claim may not have been poetic licence; he maintained to the end of his days (for example, in a letter to his publisher Mr Murray) that he had scored a total of 18 in the match. It is highly possible that the scorers, confused no doubt by the presence of a runner, awarded several of Byron's notches, by literary coincidence, to Shakespeare. The runner was Stratford Canning, later Lord Stratford de Redcliffe. Runners are permitted today only for batsmen injured during the match.

The anti-Byron school can however point to the statement of the Harrow captain of 1808, Charles Lloyd, who is quoted in Dean Merivale's *Recollections* with the following ungracious comments: 'Byron played in the Eleven, and very badly too. He should never have been in the Eleven had my counsel been taken.' This seems a rather harsh judgement, even if Byron had only made 7 and 2, considering the overall Harrow performance. He certainly bowled one Etonian and may have obtained other wickets, but bowlers' names were not then recorded if the batsman was dismissed by a catch.

The principal interest today in this contemporary record of the first ever Eton–Harrow match at Lord's is not that Eton won by an innings and 2 runs but that Lord Byron (batting with a runner because of his club foot) played for Harrow, scoring 7 and 2. Perhaps displaying an early flowering of the inventiveness that characterized his work in manhood, Byron wrote in a letter just after the match that:

When William Ward purchased the lease of Lord's Cricket Ground from its founder in 1825, he did much more than rescue a green from the threat of builders. It is probable that the MCC itself would have suffered damage beyond measure had their recently established headquarters of cricket been taken from them for a third time. With the support of the club's first Honorary Secretary, Benjamin Aislabie, Ward as proprietor and his fellow committee members improved the facilities and the finances of the club and ground with admirable zest. A fire destroyed the pavilion in July 1825, but by the start of the 1826 season Ward had opened a new building. In 1835, however, personal cash problems compelled him to transfer the lease of Lord's, which had just over 58 years to run, to James Henry Dark. Ward continued to serve as a committee member (he was on the Committee from 1826 to 1841, and again in 1845) and retained an active interest in the ground until his death in 1849. Dark paid £2000 for the lease and undertook to pay an annuity of £425 during the unexpired team.

Dark remained proprietor of the ground for almost thirty years. As had Ward, he kept the builders at bay. He began his sporting career as a groundboy at the Dorset Square Lord's, only ten years old when first engaged to field to practising members. He became a fine cricketer and represented the Players against the Gentlemen in 1835. He was also a noted umpire. He was a reticent, sometimes short-tempered man, remembered during his time at Lord's (which was often referred to as 'Dark's' during his tenure) primarily as a generous person, dedicated to the well-being of the ground, the club and the game. He collected a considerable number of oil paintings, which were acquired by the MCC in 1867.

In 1860, the Eyre Estate sold the freehold of Lord's at public auction. Dark was among many who attempted to persuade the MCC that they should bid, but they 'very unwisely' (Sir Pelham Warner) declined. The club's extraordinary lack of foresight over this and other contemporary issues such as the legalization of overarm bowling brought the MCC enormous criticism from county clubs and threatened its very survival. Lord's was purchased by Mr Isaac Moses for £7000. Three years later, Dark offered to sell his unexpired lease (just under thirty years still to run) to the club. This set off a series of negotiations between the MCC, Dark (in failing health) and Moses (who changed his name to Marden). These did not always run smoothly, but the appointment in 1863 of the forward-looking R. A. Fitzgerald as MCC Secretary was a major factor in dragging the club into the second half of the nineteenth century. Moses/Marden was reapproached and an offer made for the freehold. He wanted over £18,000 for the property he had purchased for £7000 six years before, but the MCC was at last totally aware of the vital importance of controlling their own headquarters, and the deal was struck. On 22 August 1866, Lord's became their property. Under Fitzgerald, the club moved swiftly to restore its authority in the cricket world.

This engraving appeared in the
Sporting Magazine in 1793 and is
the only authentic picture of
cricket on Thomas Lord's first
ground, at Dorset Square, of which
he was tenant from 1787 until
1810.

6

LORD'S
1793
Engraving 3½″ × 5″

———————— 7 ————————

WARD, William
(1787–1849)
Lithograph by W. Walton after
W. Drummond
Printed by M. and N. Hanhart
Published by W. H. Mason and
Robert Dark, 1849

William Ward purchased the
Lord's lease in 1825. In 1820 he
had scored 278 for the MCC
against Norfolk at Lord's, an
individual total which was not
exceeded there until 1925 (by
Percy Holmes). He was also one of
the best-known financiers of his
generation, being elected a director
of the Bank of England in 1817.
He later became Tory MP for the
City of London.

———————— 8 ————————

WARD, William
(1787–1849)
Cricket ball, 9″ circumference, 5¼ oz
No legible maker's mark

This is the ball with which Ward
scored his 278 for the MCC at
Lord's, 24–26 July 1820. His
innings began on his 33rd
birthday. It was not only the
highest score recorded at Lord's at
that time but the highest recorded
in all first-class cricket.

Benjamin Aislabie was the first Secretary of the MCC, a post he held from 1822 until 1842; he was President in 1823. A large, easy-going Old Etonian, whose bulk in later years would have tested the sturdiest of horses, he played 55 first-class matches for four counties and the MCC, winding up with a career batting average of just 3.20. He wrote many cricket songs and poems but not this one, of which he is the subject:

He doats on the game, has played many a year,

Weighs at least seventeen stone, on his pins rather queer;
But he still takes the bat, and there's no better fun
Than to see him when batting attempting a run

The hard work and devotion to the club of Aislabie during his forty years as a member won him great affection within the MCC. He was a most popular after-dinner speaker and often went further by singing his own cricket songs and verses at Anniversary Dinners. He is mentioned in *Tom Brown's Schooldays*: 'Old Mr Aislabie

———— 9 ————

AISLABIE, Benjamin
(1774–1842)
Oil on canvas 28″ × 36″
W. Novice, 1814

stood by looking on in his white hat, leaning on a bat, in benevolent enjoyment.'

William Novice (*fl.* 1809–33) exhibited five pictures at the Royal Academy between the above dates but only one, 'The Blacksmith's Shop', has any sporting link. His figure painting is more distinguished than his horse portraiture.

The walls of Lord's are the distinguished backdrop to many portraits of men whose contribution to the game is not measured by cricketing ability alone. The officers of the MCC – presidents, secretaries, treasurers, even mere committee men – were much more than servants to a private club: for the century following the purchase of their own ground, cricket itself was in their hands; their power extended around the world.

It was only in the late 1960s that the MCC's pre-eminence in English cricket began to disappear: first because of the creation of the National Cricket Association in 1966 – a body formed to oversee all cricket other than first-class; and then as a result of the establishment of the Test and County Cricket Board, created in 1968, which now runs all first-class cricket and overseas tours by English teams. The MCC is today merely part of a structure known as the Cricket Council, along with the NCA and the TCCB, but it retains control and copyright of the *Laws* (last revised in 1980) and of course remains the owner of the most celebrated cricket ground in the world. None the less the MCC is in demand – the length of the waiting list means that those proposed for membership today, unless they can qualify by proving their worth on the field of play, are scheduled to wait for several years before they can join the fortunate 18,000.

Lord Harris is without doubt one of the most important figures in cricketing history. He had his first net at Lord's in 1862 and played his last game there 67 years later. He was seventy-nine when he last played at Eton, for whom he first played before going up to Oxford where he was three times a Blue, in 1871, 1872 and 1874. He played for Kent from 1870 to 1911, and captained England in all his four Test matches, including the first Test ever played in England, against Australia at The Oval in 1880. He was a forceful batsman, a brilliant fielder and a useful change bowler. His best year was 1864 when he hit 1417 runs at 33.73.

For all his achievements as a player, his greatest work in cricket was carried out as an administrator, official and guardian of the game's laws and disciplinary codes. From the time he became captain of Kent in 1871, he dominated and dramatically improved that county's fortunes. He was President of Kent in 1875, Honorary Secretary from 1875 to 1880, and for most of his life a committee member. No important decision was taken there without his concurrence for the best part of sixty years. Beyond Kent, he proved to be as influential a personality at Lord's, holding various MCC offices, including the Presidency in 1895. He was a Trustee from 1906 to 1916 and Honorary Treasurer from 1916 until his death.

His adherence to the *Laws of Cricket* and to the rules governing the game's administration was punctilious, if not obsessive. More than one cricketer, including the young Walter Hammond, found his livelihood threatened by Harris's rigorous investigations into his qualification to play for a particular team.

The 1880 Test at The Oval might never have taken place without his determined organization. Among campaigns he successfully fought was that to eliminate the throwing epidemic in the 1880s, even when this meant taking action against Kent bowlers. Beyond cricket, he was at various times Under-Secretary of India, Under-Secretary for War and Governor of Bombay, Lord-in-Waiting to Queen Victoria and ADC to Kings Edward VII and George V.

10

LORD HARRIS
(The Hon. George Robert Canning)
(1851–1932)
(4th Baron, of Seringapatam and
Mysore, and of Belmont, Kent)
Bronze bust, 13¾″ high, 11½″ wide
Artist unknown, presumably late
nineteenth century

This portrait of Lord Harris wearing the bow tie of the Band of Brothers, was commissioned by the MCC for £300. The Band of Brothers is one of the most famous cricket clubs of Kent, the oldest of all county wandering sides, founded in 1858.

11

LORD HARRIS
(The Hon. George Robert Canning)
(1851–1932)
Oil on canvas, 36″ × 28″
Arthur Hacker RA, 1919

F. E. Lacey was Secretary of the MCC for 28 years from 1898; at the end of his tenure of this post he was knighted for services to the game – the first cricketing knighthood. He played first-class cricket for Hampshire from 1880 to 1897 as a middle-order batsman and slow bowler, but his greatest cricketing feat occurred in a Minor Counties match in 1887 when he scored 323 not out for Hampshire against Norfolk – still the record individual score in a Minor Counties game. He was a barrister and ruled the MCC Secretariat with stern efficiency. He is portrayed here at Lord's in morning dress.

12

LACEY, Sir Francis Eden
(1859–1946)
Oil on canvas 16½″ × 12½″
English school, c. 1900

———————— 13 ————————

THE FOUNDERS OF I ZINGARI

Sir Spencer Ponsonby-Fane
(1824–1915) (*left*)

John Loraine Baldwin
(1815–95) (*in wheelchair*)

The Earl of Bessborough
(1809–96) (*right*)

Oil on canvas 61″ × 58″

English school, 1897

I Zingari (the name is Italian for 'The Gypsies') is the oldest surviving wandering cricket club. It was founded in 1845 by the three men in this picture, together with R. P. Long, at a supper at the Blenheim Hotel, Bond Street, London. When at Cambridge, F. Ponsonby (later Frederick, 6th Earl of Bessborough), C. G. Taylor, W. Bolland and others devoted their leisure moments to cricket and to theatricals. From these interests sprang many combinations of cricket matches and theatrical events which in 1842 became a central part of what is now the Canterbury Week, and led to the creation of the Old Stagers, the oldest amateur theatrical company in the world, who perform every year during the Week.

Frederick, his brother S. Ponsonby (later the Rt Hon. Sir Spencer Ponsonby-Fane*), J. L. Baldwin and R. P. Long informed Bolland the day after the dinner that he was Perpetual President of I Zingari, and twenty of their friends that they were members. The 'Rules and Regulations' make it clear that the club was designed as much for social and personal association as it was for cricket. The cricketing aims were 'to encourage country cricket and amateur bowling; to ensure which no professionals are to play for us'; and the qualifications for membership were to be 'not only a good cricketer but a good fellow'.

The famous colours of red, black and gold were adopted after the club's first 'Liberal Legal Advisor', Tom Taylor (later the editor of *Punch*), who was writing a history of gypsies, returned from Bohemia with some gypsy handkerchiefs of those colours, said to symbolize 'an ascent out of darkness, through fire, into light'. I Zingari, while retaining only a small active membership, has flourished beyond its founders' greatest expectations for nearly 150 years; even back in 1904 Sir Spencer said on the occasion of a dinner to mark his eightieth birthday: 'We never imagined the club would assume the mammoth proportions which it has at present.' The club's aim of encouraging amateur cricket was totally successful in that many other distinguished clubs were founded on similar principles – the Free Foresters, the Quidnuncs and the Harlequins being among them.

Sir Spencer Ponsonby-Fane alone of the three founders played first-class cricket, for the MCC, Surrey and Middlesex, between 1841 and 1864. He joined the MCC in 1840 and was Treasurer from 1879 until his death. He was on several occasions invited to become President, but he always declined. He laid the foundation stone of the present Pavilion in 1889. He was also the initiator of the club's art collection in 1864 – now, as it is hoped this book illustrates, the most important cricket collection in the world.

*An anonymous poet penned these lines about Sir Spencer's name-expansion:

> . . . He who (*why* I can't explain)
> To honoured name of Ponsonby has added Fane

'Gubby' Allen has been one of the most influential men at Lord's for many years. From 1955 to 1961 he was Chairman of the Test Selectors, and was President of the MCC in 1963, Treasurer from 1964 to 1976. As a fast bowler and a forceful middle- to late-order batsman, he played 25 times for England, captaining his country against India at home in 1936 and on two overseas tours, to Australia in 1936–7, and to the West Indies in 1947–8 at the age of forty-five. He played for Eton, Cambridge University and Middlesex, taking all ten wickets in an innings at Lord's for his county against Lancashire for 40 runs in 1929. Although part of Jardine's fast attack in Australia during the 'Bodyline' tour of 1932–3, he refused to bowl leg theory. In 1986 he was knighted for his services to cricket.

In addition to this bust, by the son of former Northamptonshire and England wicket-keeper Keith Andrew, a portrait of Sir George Allen, painted in 1969 by J. Ward, hangs in the Long Room.

14

ALLEN, Sir George Oswald Browning
CBE
(1902–   )
Bronze bust 17½″ high, 13½″ wide,
11½″ deep
Neale Andrew, 1986

Colonel R. S. Rait Kerr was Secretary of the MCC from 1936 to 1952, although when during the years of the Second World War his Army duties naturally took him away from Lord's, the 66-year-old Sir Pelham Warner occupied his seat with the title Deputy Assistant-Secretary. Rait Kerr was a man of astounding efficiency whose minutes were matchless and whose reorganisation of MCC's internal governing structure vital. He supervised the post-war revision of the Laws which resulted in the Code of 1947. He played six first-class cricket matches, for the Army and other teams. He published a book tracing the history of the Laws. His daughter Diana was for many years the Curator at Lord's. This is a posthumous portrait.

15

RAIT KERR, Colonel Rowan Scrope
CBE, DSO, MC
(1891–1961)
Crayon and wash drawing on tinted
paper 19″ × 26″
John Ward RA, 1966

Ronald Aird was MCC's ninth Secretary, succeeding Colonel Rait Kerr in 1952. His time in office was one untroubled by international war or major internal dispute. For most of his era the English cricket team was pre-eminent and their solid achievements on the field were matched by solid developments at Lord's including the building of the Warner Stand and the Memorial Gallery. One of the most popular men in all cricket, he became President of the premier club in 1968. Aird won his blue at Cambridge in 1923 and played 108 first-class games for Hampshire between 1920 and 1938, primarily as a batsman.

Also seen in the picture are R. T. Gaby (Club Superintendent) and C. H. Wray (Club Accountant).

— 16 —

AIRD, Ronald, MC
(1902–1986)
Crayon and wash drawing on tinted paper 19″ × 26″
John Ward RA, 1964

This drawing of S. C. 'Billy' Griffith was executed in the year after Griffith retired as Secretary of the MCC, a post he had held for twelve years after taking over from R. Aird. He was President of the club in 1979–80. A wicket-keeper and lower-order batsman, he made his first-class debut for Cambridge University in 1934 and went on to play for Sussex from 1937 to 1954 (captain in 1946). He played in three Test matches for England, most notably against the West Indies in Trinidad in 1947–8. Picked to tour as player-manager and reserve wicket-keeper, he

found himself opening the innings in his debut Test. He proceeded to score his maiden first-class hundred – no less than 140 in six hours. Griffith's years of office at Lord's were often stormy ones, with crises such as the d'Oliveira affair, the rebuilding of the Tavern and the erosion of much of the MCC's power on the formation of the Cricket Council taking place during his time as Secretary. The fact that he subsequently rose to the Presidency is tribute to his diplomatic handling of these highly sensitive issues.

17

GRIFFITH, Stewart Cathie
CBE, DFC
(1914–)
Crayon and wash drawing on tinted paper 18″ × 24″
John Ward RA, 1975

The Lord's collection does not include a great many paintings of actual games that took place at the ground. However, in recent years the MCC commissioned paintings of both the 1980 Centenary Test Match (which commemorated 100 years of England–Australia Test matches in England) and of the Bicentenary Match of 1987 (to celebrate the club's double-century) from Arthur Weaver and William Bowyer respectively.

A total of 5551 spectators paid 2/6d each to watch the first day of the Eton *v* Harrow game at Lord's on Friday 9 July 1886, and 6193 did so on Saturday 10 July. For all that, it was the least well-attended Eton–Harrow match for five years. Eton won convincingly by six wickets, their first win since 1876, C. P. Foley scoring 114 in their first innings and H. R. Bromley-Davenport taking nine Harrow wickets in the match. Both these players went on to play for Cambridge and Middlesex, Bromley-Davenport eventually appearing four times for England. This picture shows the old pavilion (demolished in 1889) and 'A' enclosure.

By 1886 the Eton–Harrow match at Lord's had become one of the most glamorous social occasions of the year. Royalty frequently graced the event, which began to lose its lustre only after the Second World War.

Albert Chevallier Tayler (1862–1926) won a scholarship to the Slade in 1879 and studied in Paris before moving to Newlyn, Cornwall in 1884, working there on and off with Stanhope Forbes and other artists for several years. He was a lively and popular character in this circle who once left Newlyn for Venice in a state of 'high glee for he had played a cricket match in the afternoon and made top score'.

18

ETON *v* HARROW AT LORD'S
1886
Oil on canvas 12″ × 15″
A. Chevallier Tayler,
1886

His surviving work is so varied that it is hard to see a unity of theme within it. Among his other works at Lord's are a portrait of R. A. H. Mitchell (1843–1905) who three times led Oxford University to victory over Cambridge at Lord's from 1863 to 1865, and eight crayon drawings depicting cricketing notables such as Beldam, Ranjitsinhji, Rhodes and Trott (see pages 110 and 111).

This is not a picture of one particular England–Australia match at Lord's but an imaginary scene at the ground featuring many prominent players and spectators of the day. At the time of the painting there had been only two Tests played at headquarters, in 1884 and 1886.

In the picture, which looks towards the Tavern, W. G. Grace is the batsman, W. W. Read the non-striker, F. R. Spofforth the bowler and T. W. Garrett the fielder in the foreground. The Prince and Princess of Wales are seen standing at the boundary. One of the future King Edward VII's mistresses, Lillie Langtry, sitting in the old 'A' enclosure, turns her back on the royal couple.

The 22 players featured in the individual portraits never faced each other in that combination. They are:

England	*Australia*
R. G. Barlow	T. W. Garrett
W. Scotton	P. S. McDonnel
W. Barnes	S. P. Jones
A. N. Hornby	A. C. Bannerman
Hon. A. Lyttelton	H. J. H. Scott
W. G. Grace	F. R. Spofforth
A. G. Steel	G. Griffen
Lord Harris	C. F. Palmer
G. Ulyett	J. M. Blackham
W. W. Read	W. L. Murdoch
A. Shrewsbury	C. J. Bonnor

George Hamilton Barrable (fl. 1873–87) was a London painter who specialized in interior and domestic subjects. More is known of *Sir Robert Ponsonby Staples*, 12th Baronet (1853–1943), who was an Irish portrait, genre and landscape painter. He visited Australia in 1879–80. Among his many works which survive are 'The Last Shot for the Queen's Prize – Wimbledon' (1887), 'Mr

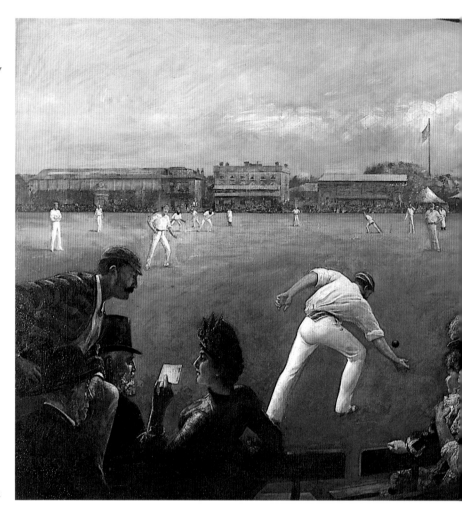

Gladstone Introducing the Home Rule Bill, 13th February 1893' and portraits of Queen Victoria and King Edward VII.

'England *v* Australia' was purchased from Sir Robert in 1927.

───────── 19 ─────────

ENGLAND *v* AUSTRALIA AT LORD'S

Oil on canvas 58″ × 117″, with 22 portraits on individual panels, mounted and framed, 10″ × 139″

G. H. Barrable and R. Ponsonby Staples, 1887

This imposing picture of the players in the field is not of any one combination that played as such towards the end of the nineteenth century, when Gents *v* Players was one of the leading national sporting fixtures, but a composite by Dickinsons featuring many of the notables of the time.

The cricketers from the left are: J. Phillips (umpire), A. Ward, A. E. Stoddart and W. G. Grace (Gents batsmen), J. T. Hearne, G. A. Lohmann, W. Gunn, A. Shrewsbury, R. Peel, R. Briggs, J. Wheeler (umpire), M. Sherwin (wicket-keeper), J. M. Read, W. H. Lockwood and W. Attewell.

20

THE PLAYERS IN THE FIELD
Lord's on a Gentlemen *v* Players Day
Oil on canvas 39½″ × 80″
Dickinsons, 1895

The Second Test in the 1938 Ashes series, 24–28 June, is the subject of this painting. Both Walter Hammond, the England captain, and Bill Brown, the Australian opening batsman, made double centuries, and Don Bradman, on his third tour of England (his first as captain), scored 102 not out in the final innings.

Charles Cundall (1890–1971), RA 1944, was the official war artist to the Royal Navy and to the Royal Air Force during the Second World War. He was a painter in oil and watercolour of landscapes, townscapes and portraits. Lancashire-born, he started out as a designer of pottery and stained glass.

The crowd in the foreground of the picture are in the 'free' seats and the 1890 pavilion majestically dominates the background. Father Time surveys the scene from the top of the Grandstand, completed in 1926, casting his shadow over the field of play.

21

ENGLAND *v* AUSTRALIA AT LORD'S
1938
Oil on canvas 42″ × 60″
Charles Cundall RA, 1938

The England–Australia Test at Lord's in 1980 was not part of an Ashes series but a single match held in September, after England had completed a full series against the West Indies, to commemorate the 100th anniversary of the first Test staged in England. The 1880 game was in fact played at The Oval but it was felt that the headquarters of cricket was the appropriate venue for the Centenary celebrations.

The match itself was a disappointment, despite two magnificent innings for Australia by Kim Hughes. Rain and an altercation between some MCC members and the umpires marred the occasion, the match ending in an unexciting draw.

Weaver's picture shows the view from the free seats at the east side of the ground, as did the Cundall 1938 picture, but from a slightly different angle. London-born *Arthur Weaver* (1918–   ) has been based in Wales since 1947. In addition to his sporting commission from the MCC, he has published a series of pictures of the world's finest golf courses. His landscape work has included commissions to paint Texan oil wells and the Williamson diamond mine in South Africa.

———————— 22 ————————

ENGLAND *v* AUSTRALIA, LORD'S
1980
Oil on canvas 27″ × 40″
Arthur Weaver, 1980

This painting was commissioned by the MCC on the occasion of the five-day match between the MCC and the Rest of the World towards the end of the 1987 season to mark the club's 200th birthday. The first four days of the game were played in splendid weather and there were many superb individual performances, notably Sunil Gavaskar's first century at Lord's. Although rain completely wiped out the last day, no damage was done to the sporting and social success of the event.

William Bowyer (1926–) was Head of Fine Art at the Maidstone College of Art from 1971 to 1982. He is an enthusiastic club cricketer who lives and works in London. His commissioned picture is painted as if from above the free seats opposite the New Mound Stand in the background.

23

THE BICENTENARY MATCH AT LORD'S
1987
Oil on canvas 39″ × 60″
William Bowyer RA, 1987

This drawing of the famous Long Room in the Lord's Pavilion portrays a scene that has remained virtually the same over the decades every time an important match takes place. The members (no outsiders may even enter the Pavilion) sit in low or high chairs, or on the tables, or simply stand quietly (by the standards of almost any other sporting crowd) watching the proceedings through the windows. Every incoming or outgoing batsman must pass through the Long Room on his journeys between dressing-room and wicket.

The Long Room is 93 feet long and 27 feet wide and on its walls and in its cabinets are many of the finest items of the Lord's art collection. The greatest achievers – Grace, Wisden, Bradman, Hobbs, Warner, Jardine and many more –

are all represented in the Long Room today. A player's pride (or his despair) as he leaves the field to face the gaze of heroes past and members present is irresistibly magnified as his boots clatter across the expansive floor.

Despite the fact that the Long Room is comparatively empty in Dennis Flanders' masterly 1953 drawing, it is possible that the game in progress was the famous England v Australia Test of that year when Willie Watson and Trevor Bailey defied the Australian attack for the best part of a day to earn England the most honourable of draws. (On the final day the crowd was a small one, as it seemed likely at the start that England would lose quickly.) There again, it could have been Middlesex v Somerset on a grey afternoon.

24

THE LONG ROOM AT LORD'S
1953
Watercolour 12½″ × 16½″
Dennis Flanders, 1953

The MCC Bicentenary celebrations of 1987 were marked by the issue of a wide variety of commemorative items, ranging from decanters to pill boxes and from scarves to prints. Former captain of England Tony Lewis was commissioned to write *Double Century* and of the many official celebratory functions, the game between the MCC and the Rest of the World was the centrepiece. Earlier generations were just as enthusiastic about such mathematically satisfying anniversaries as the following selection shows.

The inscription reads: 'Jubilee Match at Lord's of the Marylebone Club July 10th 1837'. On reverse: oval reproduction of an engraving of the North *v* South match played at Lord's on 10–11 July 1837, flanked by rose sprays.

Lt-Col R. S. Williams-Thomas of the Royal Brierly Crystal Glassworks put forward his firm to manufacture this piece.

The North, aided by southerners Box and Cobbett, scored 64 and 65; the South 60 and 70 for 5, winning by five wickets. A crowd of 3000 attended on each day and saw William Lillywhite take fourteen wickets.

25
MCC 50th anniversary goblet
Royal Brierly Crystal
Height: 7¼″; diameter: rim 4⅝″,
square base 3⅝″
Rummer, 1837
Presented by H. J. Stevenson, 1921

The quatrain on the goblet, by the celebrated writer and publisher (and MCC member) E. V. Lucas CH (1868–1938), reads:

A hundred years and fifty pass
Yet still upon Lord's primal grass
Is waged the finest war of all:
The conflict of the bat and ball

— 26 —

MCC 150th anniversary goblet
Glass
Height: 6½″; diameter: rim 3¼″, base 3½″
Designed by Barnaby Powell, engraved by William Wilson for the MCC
Manufactured at Whitefriars Glass Works, 1937

As we have seen, Thomas Lord took possession of his third and final headquarters in or around June 1813. On 2 May 1814 it was announced that 'the New Ground is completely ready for playing on'. From the very first the new Lord's was far more popular than his second property had ever been.

The bowl's decoration in black, brown and gold consists of a representation of Lord's in 1964 at the centre of the inside, surrounded by four roundels – the MCC monogram, a cameo bust of Thomas Lord, the MCC St George touring badge, and the Old Father Time weather vane – all linked by a band of oak leaves and acorns (a traditional Worcester design). On the outside, in ovals, are two scenes representing the early days at Lord's and the ground in its 75th year. Between the ovals are trophies of cricket gear in 1814 and 1964.

On the base is written: 'This bowl commemorates the 150th anniversary of Thomas Lord's third ground.'

The bowl was presented by Viscount Cobham, KG, GCMG, GCVO, in 1965.

27

150th anniversary of Lord's present ground
Bone china (Royal Worcester) bowl, *c.* 1965
4⅛″ high, 10⅛″ diameter
Designed by Neal French, painted by Harry Davis

This loving (and therefore three-handled) cup by London silversmith and MCC member Theo Fennell was commissioned by the MCC to commemorate the club's Bicentenary in 1987. The part-enamelled circular bowl, the interior of which is gilded, tapers to a pedestal foot. The three handles depict stumps, bails and half cricket balls. Below each handle is a cricket bat – one as used in 1787, one as used in 1887 and one as used in 1987. The cup sits on a plain circular silver plinth, which has three applied enamel MCC motifs and is engraved with the years 1787, 1887 and 1987.

28

MCC Bicentenary loving cup
Sterling silver
Height: 9″; diameter at top 10½″, at bottom 7″; weight: 103 troy oz
Theo Fennell, 1987

PART TWO

Eighteenth Century

The eighteenth century was the century in which cricket became an organized, codified, national sport. Both aristocrat and commoner were drawn to its athletic, aesthetic and social attributes. Games with club and ball had existed in England for hundreds of years even before the first definite reference to cricket, in a manuscript of 1598 in which 'crickett' was one of the pastimes stated to have taken place on a disputed piece of land in Guildford. By the early 1800s cricket was played on many of the estates of the great landowners, the first patrons of the game. Their employees and retainers were essential components of the teams, who would play for high stakes on each other's grounds.

Perhaps the two most significant dates in the long history of cricket are 1744 and 1787. The latter date, as we have seen, was the year in which the MCC was founded and in which Thomas Lord staged his first match, at his Dorset Square ground. In 1744 the first known issue of the *Laws* (not rules) of the game was drawn up, and that year is also the date of the first great match of which the full score is preserved: that of Kent *v* All-England, on 18 June, on the Artillery Ground, Finsbury – the ground of the Honourable Artillery Company ever since. Kent were victorious by one wicket and their triumph that day is recorded in detail by James Love in his 'Cricket: A Heroic Poem' published the same year.

The earliest known rules governing the way cricket should be played survive in the form of an agreement made on 11 July 1727 between the 2nd Duke of Richmond and Mr A. Brodrick for two matches they were to play against each other's sides that year; among stipulations that covered most aspects of the game were that 'the wickets shall be pitched at a fair and even place at twenty three yards distance from each other' and that 'a ball caught, cloathed or not cloathed, the striker is out'.

The earliest printed version of the *Laws of Cricket* was published in 1744 by the London Club and 'committee of Noblemen and Gentlemen of Kent, Surrey, Sussex, Middlesex and London'. The Club's President was Frederick Louis, Prince of Wales, father of George III, whose enthusiasm for cricket cost him the throne (see page 98).

Two stages of the evolution of the cricket bat from crude stick to the sophisticated present-day blades are shown here. The 1750 curved bat is one stage on from an instrument that resembled the modern hockey stick. The 1744 Laws did not specify any dimensions, but thirty years later the maximum width of the bat was limited to 4¼ inches. The May 1774 bat illustrated here would thus have been one of the first to have been subject to this stipulation, although the curved bat continued to be used until well into the nineteenth century. By 1827 all bats were straight and in 1840 the length was limited to 38 inches.

30

Straight bat
1774
34″ long, 4¼″ wide,
2lb 13oz

29

Curved bat
1750
37½″ long, 4″ wide,
2lb 5oz

31

MANN, Sir Horatio
(1744–1814)
Pastel painting 44″ × 36″
(On loan from Lord Cornwallis)
Hugh Douglas Hamilton, c. 1785

Sir Horatio Mann was one of cricket's greatest eighteenth-century patrons. He was MP for Maidstone from 1774 to 1784 and for Sandwich from 1790 to 1807. He played for Kent from 1773 to 1782 in an era before matches were officially designated first-class or otherwise. He hosted many important fixtures at his Dandelion, near Margate, estate and at Bishopsbourne, near Canterbury. He once organized a cricket match to be played on horseback. In this portrait he is captured in satisfied repose during one of his many other sporting pursuits.

Hugh Douglas Hamilton (1736–1808) was a prolific Irish portraitist in oils and crayon. He studied under West in Dublin from 1750 to 1756 and then moved to London in the mid-1760s. Later he was based in Rome (1778–91) where he painted many British visitors to the city, of whom Sir Horatio was one.

William Rice is believed to have been Clerk of Works at Hampton Court Palace. He is seen here posing with an oversized bat in the year of the first important match of which a full scorecard survives.

Robert Scaddon (*fl.* 1743–74) was a portrait painter who may have been a pupil of Thomas Hudson (see page 65). Note the two-stump wicket in the game being played in the distance.

32

RICE, William
Oil on canvas 65½″ × 49″
Robert Scaddon, 1744

An enchanting small painting,
whose provenance is unknown.

——— 33 ———
E. MOULTALT-MAUDE OF JERSEY
Oil on canvas 18″ × 16″
H. Kafler, date unknown

Francis Hayman's famous picture shows cricket being played in the Regent's Park area some forty years before Thomas Lord bought his first ground in what is now Dorset Square. All eleven fielders are shown in a field setting for what appears to be an aggressive batsman, that can perhaps be criticized only for a lack of mid-off and backward square leg. One can envisage the umpire near the batsman getting in the way of urgent action at the wicket-keeper's end. Scorers with their tally sticks are seen in the foreground. The wicket is a two-stump affair with the single bail resting on the forked tops of the stumps. The introduction of the third stump was still some thirty years away. The bowler, hand on knee, is about to unleash a slow but subtle underarm delivery.

Francis Hayman (1708–76) was a founder member of the Royal Academy. Like his friend Hogarth, he was a great theatre enthusiast and produced many works of and for the theatre. 'Cricket as Played in the Mary-le-Bone Fields' is a highly important article of cricketing history – certainly the most valuable illustration of the game as played in the mid-eighteenth century. Over the years

34

CRICKET AS PLAYED IN THE MARY-LE-BONE FIELDS
Oil on canvas 34″ × 43″
Francis Hayman RA, *c.* 1744

the picture (or variations of it) has been reproduced many times, notably in conjunction with late eighteenth- and early nineteenth-century editions of the *Laws of Cricket* (see also No. 35). The original was almost certainly owned by Thomas Lord, whence it passed to William Ward, and eventually to the MCC itself, along with the lease of the ground.

The scene depicted on the handkerchief is an adaptation of Francis Hayman's 'Cricket in the Mary-le-Bone Fields' (see No. 34). According to Colonel R. S. Rait Kerr, Secretary of the MCC from 1936 to 1952, in his important book *The Laws of Cricket* (1950), the handkerchief is dated about 1744, which, if correct, obviously means that the 1747 or 1748 dates sometimes attributed to the Hayman original are wrong.

35
Linen handkerchief
26½″ × 28½″
c. 1744
Presented by J. W. Goldman

The picture by an unknown painter shows a game taking place in a Surrey meadow along the edge of which runs the River Mole. The house of the celebrated actor David Garrick is seen on the left. Many important eighteenth-century matches were staged at Moulsey Hurst. In 1723 the future King George II entertained the London and Surrey teams at Hampton Court after a match at the ground. His son, Frederick Louis, Prince of Wales, was a most enthusiastic cricketer. The *Grub Street Journal* of 29 May 1735 announced:

His Royal Highness the Prince has made a very considerable match of cricket to be played on Saturday June 7, at Moulsey Hurst. His Royal Highness takes the County of Surrey against Esquire Steed and the London Club. There are already upwards of £1500 depending.

Mr Steed's side won handsomely, some of the Prince's men being publicly branded as 'bunglers'. (See also page 56).

36

CRICKET AT MOULSEY HURST
Oil on canvas 28″ × 49″
English school, *c.* 1790

This delightful portrait of the fourteen-year-old William Wheatley, who never became a distinguished cricketer, was painted when he was a schoolboy at Charterhouse. He later served in the 1st Foot Guards and became a Major-General. Alleyne painted the entire Wheatley family, of Lesney House, Kent, in 1786: father, mother and each of the two children.

37

WHEATLEY, William
(1771–1812)
Oil on panel, oval portrait 14″ × 11″
Francis Alleyne, 1786

The Courtenay family came from Powderham Castle, Devon, where there are many portraits of the family by Hudson. The two boys here are believed to be William, born 1738, and Henry, born 1741, sons of Henry Courtenay MP, the fourth son of the 6th Earl of Devon. Henry junior became Bishop of Exeter.

Thomas Hudson (1701–79) was a leading portrait painter of his day (sitters included George II and Handel), and also a notable teacher and writer. His massive picture 'The Family of the Third Duke of Marlborough', which hangs at Blenheim Palace, appears to have been copied in part by the painter of the Courtenay brothers.

There is a certain weakness in the right arm of the younger boy which may be the work of a studio assistant.

—————— 38 ——————

THE COURTENAY BROTHERS
Oil on canvas 56″ × 48″
Thomas Hudson, *c.* 1751

Thomas Hope was a student of architecture, a designer and fine arts collector, the eldest son of an English merchant based in Amsterdam and his Dutch wife. He settled in England after the French occupation of Holland. This portrait by the Swiss painter

Jacques Sablet (1749–1803) was, however, executed in Rome during Hope's grand tour of Europe. Mount Vesuvius is alleged to be the mountain in the background.

The picture was at one time credited to Sablet's brother Jean François (1751–1819).

39

MR THOMAS HOPE OF AMSTERDAM
(1769–1831)
Playing cricket with his friends
Oil on canvas 24½″ × 19¾″
Jacques Sablet, 1792

In 1807 Thomas Hope (see page 66) acquired the country house and one hundred acre estate of the Deepdene, near Dorking in Surrey for £9030. He preferred the pursuit of intellectual to sporting entertainment at his impressive property which he expanded in irregular and spectacular style.

40

A CRICKET MATCH ON
COTMANDENE DORKING

Oil on canvas 31¾″ × 52″
James Canter, *c.* 1770

This is certainly an eighteenth-century treasure of Lord's, even if at first sight there appears to be little reason for it to hang in the Museum. Pallone ('the large ball') is a game of Italian origin, with some features in common with tennis. Up to four players are permitted on each side. There is a real tennis court at Lord's, built in 1838, one of only two dozen or so in the country, in great demand by MCC members; and pallone itself has been played at Lord's, according to A. L. Fisher's book of 1865, *The Game of Pallone*. He says:

At this time, about 1852–3, there was a great number of Italian refugees in London, many of whom could play the game of Pallone. I took advantage of this circumstance . . . I was able to have the game played at Lord's Cricket Ground.

The exhibition was apparently well received, but when Fisher attempted to organize a repeat performance, he found that most of the Italians he had recruited had left the country. Pallone never reappeared at Lord's.

In Fabris' painting, a game is taking place in the moat which used to follow the old walls of Aragon. Ferdinand I of the Two Sicilies married Maria Carolina of Austria in the probable year of the work and it is almost certainly she who appears in the box.

41

A GAME OF PALLONE AT NAPLES
Oil on canvas 29″ × 50½″
Pietro Fabris, *c.* 1768

The greatest cricketing heroes of the eighteenth century were the band of men that constituted the Hambledon Club, Broad Halfpenny (by 1782 of Windmill Down), Hampshire. The exact date of the formation of the club is not known, but from its probable creation time of the late 1750s through to 1787, cricket developed at a remarkable rate in its famous cradle. The immortal names of Hambledon include Richard Nyren, father of John (see page 71), William Beldham (see page 72), John Small, William Hogsflesh, Richard Purchase, David Harris (see pages 75 and 148), John Wells and Thomas Walker (see page 75). Their colours were sky-blue coats with black velvet collars and velvet caps.

John Nyren of Hambledon gave his name to one of the earliest classics of cricket literature, 'The Young Cricketer's Tutor and the Cricketers of My Time', in which the heroic deeds of the Hambledon players were recorded. Nyren's thoughts and tales were 'collected and edited' by the distinguished writer Charles Cowden Clarke, the book not actually appearing until 1833. An early example of a cricketing ghost writer!

Nyren's father Richard was one of the driving forces, as both captain and secretary, of the Hambledon Club, which for thirty years or so, from around 1750 until the power focus of the game switched to the MCC and Thomas Lord's first ground, was the centre of the cricketing world. John Nyren himself was an accomplished professional batsman who played first-class cricket in the early days of the nineteenth century.

42

NYREN, John
(1764–1837)
Oil on canvas 12½″ × 9½″
English school, c. 1805

Although this painting dates from the latter half of the nineteenth century, its distinguished subject is one of the last links with the Hambledon era. 'Silver Billy' was considered the game's finest batsman in his day. He was a late arrival to the Hambledon scene, whose greatest days had begun around 1770, but before the turn of the century he had become one of the renowned side's immortals, famed for his attacking play. From 1801 he began playing for Surrey, also turning out on occasion for Kent. His last important match was for Godalming in 1821.

43

BELDHAM, William
(1766–1862)
Oil on canvas 30″ × 25″
A. Vincent, c. 1860

The inn (still in operation today) at Hambledon, where the famous club was based. Richard Nyren took over the 'Bat and Ball' in 1763.

44

HAMBLEDON, THE OLD BAT AND BALL INN, Broad Halfpenny Down
Oil on canvas 16″ × 20″
English school, *c.* 1780

45

TWELVE CRICKETERS IN
CHARACTERISTIC ATTITUDES
Pen and watercolour 8″ × 10″
George Shepheard, c. 1795

Shepheard's studies of famous cricketers include the only known pictures of some of the great Hambledon players in action. We see William Beldham (see page 72), David Harris (1755–1803), recognized as the greatest bowler of his generation, and Thomas Walker. Walker (1762–1831) was the most famous defensive batsman of his day, in one game scoring just 1 run from 170 Harris deliveries.

Also featured are other important eighteenth-century figures such as Lord Frederick Beauclerk (1773–1850), the man who is considered to have succeeded Beldham as the country's finest bat. He was an accomplished all-rounder and as such an outstanding single-wicket player. This variation of the game, in which individuals compete against each other rather than as part of a team, was very popular in the late eighteenth century and attracted an enormous amount of betting. Lord Frederick lost no opportunity to turn his sporting abilities to his financial advantage. As one of the first members of the MCC, he became a powerful and autocratic force in the running of cricket. He was known to have had a foul temper. Then we also see General the Hon. Edward Bligh (1769–1840), a fine amateur bat; the Hon. Charles Lennox (later Duke of Richmond) (1764–1819), a wicket-keeper/batsman who died in Canada after being bitten by a dog; and Thomas Lord himself.

George Shepheard (1769–1842) was a painter, watercolourist and engraver, who (apart from these cricketing portraits) is best known for his English landscapes.

PART THREE

Nineteenth Century

Just as the eighteenth was the century in which cricket became an established national game, so the nineteenth was that in which it became a worldwide pursuit, highly organized, highly professional and hugely popular, crossing boundaries of country, class and creed. Its most famous personality, W. G. Grace, was a better-known personality than any man in England and, apart from Queen Victoria, than any woman either. By the year of the MCC's centenary (1887), the club (now 3216 strong) was inviolate at the head of the cricket world, controlling every aspect of the game at home and in the Empire, on the field and off.

The nineteenth century saw the formation of the County Championship and the foundation of all of today's seventeen First-Class County clubs, the first overseas tours and Test matches (England against Australia and, later, South Africa) and the spread of first-class cricket within these distant territories, the first Eton *v* Harrow and Oxford *v* Cambridge fixtures, the introduction of round-arm bowling, and dramatic evolution in the laws, dress and equipment of the game. John Wisden's *Almanack* was launched in 1864. The cricket of 1900 was much closer to the game of today, despite some of the revolutions of recent times, than it was to that of 1800.

At Lord's itself, the changes of the century were also profound. As we have seen, Thomas Lord finally arrived at the current ground in 1814. The fire that destroyed the first pavilion occurred in 1825, but thanks to the dynamism of William Ward, by then the ground's owner, a new pavilion was in its place for the following season. The first scoreboard was installed in 1846, and the first practice nets in 1865. The MCC at last obtained ownership of their own ground in 1866;

Middlesex first played there in 1877, and the Australians a year later. The first Lord's Test match was staged in 1884, three years before the club's centenary. In 1889 work began on the current Pavilion, a monument of russet and white Victorian elegance, designed by F. T. Verity.

Other famous grounds, such as Trent Bridge, Nottingham, and The Oval, south London, came into being during this period. Clubs, great and small, fixed and wandering, proliferated. Cricketing expressions and terms found their way into the English language; the game became a symbol of its creator country, a link between the nations of the Empire and a synonym for fair play.

In 1846, William Clarke of Nottingham, founder of the Trent Bridge Cricket Ground after his marriage in 1837 to the widow who kept the Trent Bridge Inn, formed his All-England XI, with himself at its head. The objectives were financial as much as they were sporting, and in both departments Clarke was supremely successful, although none of his professionals came near to earning the sums of money from the enterprise that Clarke himself stashed away. Bickering over pay with their master eventually led to the defection of most of his players.

From 1846 to 1853 Clarke (in his late forties and early fifties) took 2385 wickets – a staggering tally, even when the shortcomings of some of the opposition are taken into account. He led a team of stars – Mynn, Parr and Hillyer are all seen in individual portrait elsewhere in this book (see pages 80, 81 and 84), and other great players alongside them in this picture include James Dean of Sussex, who often bowled and kept wicket in alternate overs, and the artist of the picture himself. John Wisden (see pages 82–4) and the Sussex wicket-keeper Thomas Box were other regulars.

Felix was of Flemish descent, born Nicholas Wanostrocht. His gifts were many, both as artist and sportsman. He took over the running of a school in Camberwell at the age of nineteen, when his father, the headmaster, died unexpectedly. He played for Kent in the 1830s and appeared many times for the Gentlemen against the Players. He was also a talented musician, and as author published an instructional work, *Felix on the Bat*. On top of all this he designed a primitive bowling machine for use in schools and pioneered tubular india-rubber batting gloves. The talent that won him a place in Clarke's All-England XI, however, was solely his cricketing one. He was a left-handed all-rounder.

The All-England XI in the picture are, from the left: Joseph Guy, Parr, William Martingell, Mynn, W. Denison (cricket writer), Dean, Clarke, Felix, O. C. Pell, Hillyer, William Lillywhite, William Dorrinton, Fuller Pilch, Thomas Sewell.

46

THE ALL-ENGLAND ELEVEN
1847
Pencil and watercolour
18¼″ × 23¾″
Felix (Nicholas Wanostrocht), 1847

47

MYNN, Alfred
(1807–61)
Oil on canvas 32″ × 25½″
William Bromley, *c.* 1850

48

PARR, George
(1826–91)
Oil on canvas 30″ × 24″
William Bromley, *c.* 1850

49

WISDEN, John
(1826–84)
Oil on canvas 31½″ × 25½″
William Bromley, c. 1850

Alfred Mynn was known as the 'Lion of Kent', which county he represented from 1834 to 1859. He also played a few games for Sussex. Considered the greatest all-rounder of his time, he was a powerful right-handed batsman and a fast right-handed round-arm bowler. He appeared twenty times for the Gentlemen against the Players. The death of this popular man inspired the following epitaph by William Jeffrey Prowse:

> With his tall and stately presence,
>   with his nobly moulded form
> His broad hand was ever open,
>   his brave heart was ever warm.
> All were proud of him, all loved
>   him. As the changing seasons
>   pass,
> As our champion lies a-sleeping
>   underneath the Kentish grass,
> Proudly, sadly, we will name him
>   – to forget him were a sin;
> Lightly lie the turf on thee, kind
>   and manly Alfred Mynn.

George Parr of Nottinghamshire took over the leadership of the All-England XI from its founder William Clarke, when the latter died in 1856. The 'Lion of the North' also captained his county from 1856 to 1870 and led touring teams to North America in 1859 and to Australia and New Zealand in 1863–4. Around 1860 he was regarded as England's premier batsman. His many massive hits at Trent Bridge were commemorated by 'Parr's Tree', an elm within the ground that suffered many blows from his mighty heaves to leg. Parr's assaults it survived, but the tree finally perished in a gale in 1976.

Wisden is one of the most famous names in all sport. Born in Brighton, **John Wisden** played most of his first-class cricket for Sussex from 1845 to 1863, though he also appeared for Middlesex and Kent and toured the United States and Canada with George Parr's side in 1859, two years before the first English team (under H. H. Stephenson) went to Australia. With James Dean, he founded the United All-England XI. He was a fast right-arm off-break bowler whose greatest day on the field was his taking of all ten wickets for North *v* South at Lord's in 1850 – all his victims being bowled. He is, however, best remembered as the founder of the famous *Almanack*, which he first published in 1864. *Wisden's Cricketers' Almanack* has appeared every year since then, not even skipping a beat during the World Wars, despite a lack of both first-class cricket and paper.

Some entertaining personal recollections of Wisden were published in the 1913 edition of the *Almanack* that bears his name. This was the 'Jubilee Edition', the fiftieth. Sir Kenelm Digby, a captain of Harrow School's eleven, recalled Wisden's period of engagement as Harrow's professional bowler from 1852 to 1855: 'I have the pleasantest recollection of his quiet, modest and unassuming character, his unfailing good temper, his keenness in and enjoyment of his work, his genial disposition which made him a great favourite with all the present and former members of the school.' Sir Spencer Ponsonby-Fane (see page 35) said of him: 'I believe he was the first of the players to play in a straw hat, instead of the white topper worn by the older players.' And Canon McCormick: 'Wisden was small of stature, but well made. He bowled moderately fast and was as fair a round-arm bowler as could be seen. The best balls he bowled broke back slightly, and his style of delivery tended to make them shoot.' The Canon managed to work an account of one of his own great successes (sixteen wickets in a match) into his tribute, but ended by getting back to the subject: 'Wisden has left a very good record as a cricketer and a pleasant memory as a sportsman, a companion, a friend.' Wisden's bowling was clearly his outstanding gift; but the Reverend H. B. Biron recalled that '. . . centuries, which these days are as common as blackberries, were very rare in Wisden's time, but he scored 100 against Kent in 1850 – his innings including four 6s, and these against Willsher, than whom a better or more difficult bowler never lived'.

William Bromley III was a London historical and genre painter. He exhibited at the Society of British Artists, British Institution and the Royal Academy, 1844 to 1870.

—————— 50 ——————
HILLYER, William
(1813–61)
Pencil and wash drawing 34″ × 23″
John Corbet Anderson, 1852

—————— 51 ——————
WISDEN, John
(1826–84)
Pencil and wash drawing 34″ × 23″
John Corbet Anderson, 1852

William Hillyer was a formidable right-handed medium fast round-arm bowler, considered by many of his day to be 'the best of all bowlers', as well as being a forceful bat and an outstanding slip. He played for Kent, the county of his birth, from 1835 to 1853, and also for Surrey. In 1845 he took 174 wickets. Poor health caused his retirement, and he died aged forty-seven after a long illness.

John Corbet Anderson (1827–1907) painted a series of watercolour portraits of cricketers in the 1850s which were published as lithographs. Highly popular in their time, they are much sought-after collectors' items today.

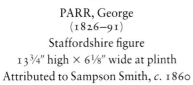

52

PARR, George
(1826–91)
Staffordshire figure
13¾″ high × 6⅛″ wide at plinth
Attributed to Sampson Smith, *c.* 1860

53

CAESAR, Julius
(1830–78)
Staffordshire figure
14″ high × 5⅞″ wide at plinth
Attributed to Sampson Smith, *c.* 1860

Julius Caesar was a leading
professional from 1849 to 1867,
an all-rounder who turned out
primarily for Surrey. He always
demanded that his full name
should appear in the scorebook.
He played for Clarke's All-England
XI, toured North America with
Parr's side in 1859 (see page 83),
and Australia in 1863–4.

At Lord's there are many highly absorbing mid-nineteenth-
century pictures not devoted to specific heroes: landscapes,
studies of village and city grounds, portraits of anonymous
youth and age – each part of the evocative backdrop of
English cricket in its adolescence.

The fielding side is wearing the colours of the Oxfordshire Bullingdon Club. The church in the background is the Augustinian Priory Church. On the right can be seen the Castle ruins. The exact site of the match is to the east of Christchurch, between Stanpit Marsh and Purewell.

54

CRICKET MATCH AT
CHRISTCHURCH, HAMPSHIRE
Oil on canvas 22″ × 32½″
English School

It is stated of this picture that it 'possibly depicts Edge Hill ground of Liverpool Cricket Club'.

―――――――― 55 ――――――――
Oil on canvas 26½″ × 44½″
W. J. Bowden, 1852

Charles and Henry Shayer (fl. 1870–80) are little-known Southampton painters who exhibited only once in London. They specialized in landscapes and sporting scenes. It is likely that they are related to the more celebrated Southampton artist William Shayer (1788–1879).

56

VILLAGE CRICKET
Oil on canvas 24″ × 42″
Charles and Henry Shayer,
c. 1870

The exact venue of the village
game pictured here by *John Ritchie*
(*fl.* 1855–75) is not known, but
date and scene suggest southern
England. Ritchie was a landscape
painter who also specialized in
imaginary scenes set in sixteenth-
or seventeenth-century costume.

57

VILLAGE CRICKET
Oil on canvas 31½″ × 49½″
John Ritchie, 1855

One of the most famous of all cricket paintings was executed by the Nottinghamshire artist *Robert James* (*fl.* 1841–51), who specialized in studies of children, in this case four Nottingham chimney-sweeps. Other versions of the painting are known and a study by James for 'Tossing for Innings' is also in the Lord's collection.

58

TOSSING FOR INNINGS
Oil on canvas 44″ × 35½″
Robert James, *c.* 1841

The jovial character portrayed here is William Davies, scorer to the Lewes Priory Cricket Club and to Sussex County Cricket Club. One of his scorebooks is kept in the MCC Library. He appears unconcerned by the gathering gloom behind him, even if the potential distractions to his work in front of him might have concerned players hoping for an accurate record. However, the fact that the stumps are lying in front of his portable table indicates that play for the day has ended and therefore his tipple is no cause for alarm. Other vital pieces of equipment, such as a tape for measuring the pitch, were entrusted to his care.

Thomas Henwood (fl. 1840–58) was a Sussex artist who provided most of the artwork for Horsfield's *History of Sussex*.

59

THE SCORER
Oil on millboard 14″ × 12″
Thomas Henwood, 1842

Garland's wonderfully extravagant painting shows the celebrations of the Excelsior Cricket Club of Islington, as their hero of the hour is carried off by his colleagues and supporters. The atmosphere is more that of a battlefield than of a field of play.

Henry Garland was a Winchester-based landscape painter, who exhibited at the Royal Academy regularly from 1854 to 1890.

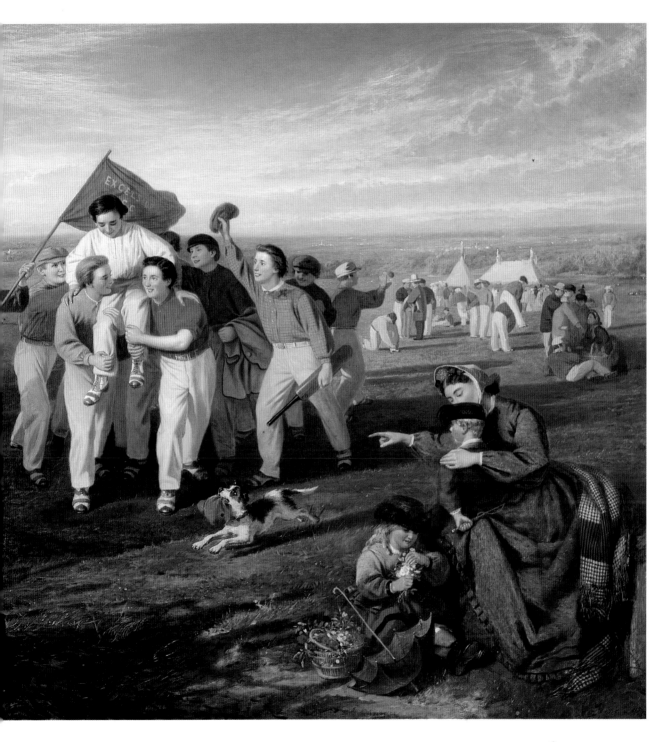

—————— 60 ——————
THE WINNER OF THE MATCH
Oil on canvas 31″ × 53″
Henry Garland, *c*. 1864

———— **61** ————

KENNINGTON OVAL
The Tavern and Entrance
Oil on canvas 12½″ × 16½″
Harry Williams, *c.* 1858

Two studies of what is today London's second Test match ground and the home of Surrey County Cricket Club.

Originally a market garden, The Oval was first prepared for cricket by Montpelier CC in 1844 and in the following year the Surrey Club organized their first fixture there. In 1845, too, the Surrey County Cricket Club was officially inaugurated. The pavilion was extended in 1858 (the probable year of these pictures) to include a clubroom with dressing-rooms behind.

Harry Williams (*fl.* 1854–77) was a Liverpool landscape painter who exhibited twice at the Royal Academy. He specialized in landscapes and coastal scenes around Liverpool and North Wales. He came to London, where he eventually died in poverty.

62

KENNINGTON OVAL
The Ground and Pavilion
Oil on canvas 12½″ × 16½″
Harry Williams, *c.* 1858

BOWL'D OUT or the K—G & All England against the Boroughmongers.

The Duke of Wellington, leader of the Tories, is shown comprehensively dismissed hit wicket as a result of a full toss labelled 'Reform' delivered by King William IV. The King was not known for great interest in cricket, although he did donate £20 to an appeal launched by Sussex in the year of his death (1837). His grandfather Frederick Louis, Prince of Wales, son of George II, was passionate about the game, which sad to say cost him his life. He received a severe blow in the side from the ball while he was playing cricket on the lawn of his Buckinghamshire home in 1751. Some months later an internal abscess – 'a collection of matter' – burst and instantly suffocated him. This may have coloured William's attitude towards the game.

The cartoon was inspired by the King's agreement, on 22 April 1831, to the dissolution of Parliament after Lord Grey's Government had suffered a defeat in committee on the first Reform Bill. The spectator crying 'Foul' is Wellington supporter Lord Aberdeen, and the whiskered gent on the right is the Duke of Cumberland. The four fielders are all Whig supporters of electoral reform – Sir Francis Burdett, Grey, Lord John Russell and Lord Brougham.

63

BOWL'D OUT or THE K__G AND
ALL-ENGLAND AGAINST THE
BOROUGHMONGERS
Lithograph 8¾″ × 13¾″
C. J. Grant, 1831
Published by Tregear, Cheapside

The giants of the game in the 1800s were many, but all were eventually dwarfed by the massive persona and achievements of William Gilbert Grace, who first played in a major match in 1864. Dr W. G. Grace dominated cricket during his lifetime in a way that no other sportsman of any kind has ever done. Three-quarters of a century after his death, his features and deeds are as familiar to cricket-lovers as those of many of the modern heroes.

He was born in Downend, Bristol on 18 July 1848, the fourth of five brothers. Three, Dr E. M., G. F. and Dr Henry, also played first-class cricket, the reputation of E. M. at one time nearly as great as that of his illustrious younger brother. At fifteen, W. G. scored 32 against an All-England XI, and just before his sixteenth birthday, 170 and 56 not out for South Wales against the Gentlemen of Sussex; at seventeen he took thirteen wickets for the Gentlemen against the Players of the South. He first appeared for Gloucestershire in 1868 and by 1871, the year he became the first man to score more than 2000 runs in a season (he made 2739), he was the most famous cricketer in the land.

He remained with Gloucestershire until 1899 and during the last thirty years of the century he created many records, playing mainly for England, his county, the MCC and the Gentlemen. He hit the first first-class triple-century in 1876 and followed with a second a few days later, having scored a mere 177 in the one intervening innings. He was the first to achieve the 'double' of 1000 runs and 100 wickets in one season. In each of twenty-eight seasons he scored over 1000 runs; in eight seasons he took over 100 wickets. In 1895, when aged forty-seven, he became the first to score 1000 runs in May and the first to score 100 hundreds when he took 288 off the Somerset bowling. He scored 152 in the first ever Test match in 1880, and his 170 at The Oval against Australia six years later remained England's highest in a home Test until 1921. He captained England thirteen times, visiting Australia in 1873–4 (not first-class) and 1891–2, and North America in 1872 (not first-class).

After a dispute with Gloucestershire, Grace played much of his final first-class cricket with London County. At the age of fifty-six, in 1904, he scored his final century; four years later he played his last first-class innings, for the Gentlemen of England. He had by then scored over 50,000 first-class runs and taken nearly 3000 first-class wickets.

He was qualified as a doctor of medicine, and in his youth was a champion athlete, but cricket was his priority in life. The 'Old Man' made a large amount of money from the game, from match fees and testimonials, although he was theoretically an amateur. He was by no means averse to gamesmanship, often of the kind that causes great outrage when practised today; he had no qualms about arguing with umpires, 'sledging' (the practice of distracting opposing batsmen at crucial moments with unhelpful comment), walk-outs or bending the laws. But of course he is rightly, and most properly, revered today for his majestic mastery of the game in which he was the pre-eminent source of so much public interest for so many years. His fame was on a par with that of royalty and prime ministers; his death on 23 October 1915, as much as the Great War itself, symbolized and emphasized the passing of the Golden Age of cricket.

Grace is forever commemorated at Lord's by the Grace Gates at the Members' Entrance in St John's Wood Road, erected in July 1923, as well as by the numerous works of art that he inspired.

Of course, W. G. did not stalk the later nineteenth-century stage alone. Men such as Alfred Shaw of Nottingham, Hornby and Barlow of Lancashire, Bobby Abel of Surrey, and Peate and Peel of Yorkshire were all players who would have made their mark in any age against any opposition. But it is possible that even Grace would have shone relatively a little less brightly in the era that was ushered in with the new century.

Grace's years of dominance proved to be the overture to what is now considered cricket's Golden Age: the years preceding the First World War. As his dazzling sun slowly burned into a warm evening glow, other names that were to become immortal blazed into view. C. B. Fry, A. C. MacLaren, Tom Hayward, Kumar Shri Ranjitsinhji, Sydney Barnes, Wilfred Rhodes, Tom Richardson, G. L. Jessop, the Hon. F. S. Jackson and Jack Hobbs were just some of the Englishmen whose early careers overlapped the twilight years of the Old Man; and sailing to the mother country from 12,000 miles away, colonial stars became nearly as well known to the English public – none more so than the illustrious Victor Trumper.

This painting was commissioned by the MCC via £1 subscriptions from 1888 to 1890. Wortley (1849–1905), a popular painter of portraits and sporting subjects who studied under Millais, received £300 for the picture.

Grace is seen here in an MCC cap with the old Lord's tennis court in the background.

64

GRACE, William Gilbert
(1848–1915)
Oil on canvas 48″ × 34″
Archibald J. Stuart Wortley, 1890

Two late nineteenth-century items
of Doulton ware featuring W. G.

— 65 —

GRACE, William Gilbert
(1848–1915)
Doulton jug
9″ high, diameter 3⅝″ at rim,
5½″ at base

— 66 —

GRACE, William Gilbert
(1848–1915)
Doulton beaker
5⅛″ high, diameter 3¼″ at rim,
2¼″ at base

— 67 —

GRACE, William Gilbert
(1848–1915)
Belt and clasp
Wool on canvas/metal and gilt;
belt 2⅛″ wide, 44″ long;
clasp 2⅝″ square
c. 1870

This belt was presented to Grace
by J. H. Rawlings. On the clasp
three cricketers are framed in a
huge letter 'C' on which the
inscription continues – (C)ricket
For Ever.

GRACE, William Gilbert
(1848–1915)
London County cap
Flannel, green with narrow
yellow/red/yellow stripes;
peak *c.* 1½″
c. 1900

After his somewhat bitter
departure from Gloucestershire,
W. G.'s final seasons of regular
important cricket (1900–4) were
played with the London County
Club at Crystal Palace which,
thanks almost exclusively to
Grace, enjoyed first-class status at
this time.

—— 69 ——

GRACE, William Gilbert
(1848–1915)
Cap
Flannel, purple, red and yellow stripes
Badge: the initial 'S' purple,
surmounted by a coronet, yellow and
red
Peak: *c.* 1¼″
Label: a piece of tape, with ink
inscription – Dr W. G. Grace

This was the cap worn by W. G. as
captain of the England team to
Australia, 1891–2, the side
sponsored by Lord Sheffield. The
team lost the first two Tests, but
won the third by an innings. Lord
Sheffield was a great benefactor of
cricket, both in England and in
Australia. At the end of this tour he
donated £150 for a trophy to be
competed for by the states of New
South Wales, Victoria and South
Australia – the Sheffield Shield,
still Australia's inter-state trophy
today.

Commissioned by Grace for a dinner given by him to the Century Club, Bristol, January 1896, in return for the Club's dinner in his honour in June 1895. Each guest was presented with a plate.

1895 was a remarkable year for Grace, when he defied the years and the opinions of some rash commentators that his great deeds were all now in the past; not only did he score his 100th first-class hundred (288 *v* Somerset) which inspired the Bristol Century Club dinner, he became the first man to score 1000 runs in May and, in his forty-eighth year, outscored every other batsman in England.

70

GRACE, William Gilbert
(1848–1915)

Century of Centuries dinner plate

China (Coalport), white underglaze, 8¾″ diameter

Rim has irregular indentations (rococo design in three repeats)

Decoration: blue and gold transfers, W. G.'s signature in centre

Printed on base: a table plan of the eighteen diners

Manufactured for S. J. Keppel & Son, Bristol, 1895–6

Grace sports a forked beard and is wearing a blouse. This piece was presented to the MCC by his widow in 1919.

71

GRACE, William Gilbert
(1848–1915)
Figure – head and shoulders (over life-size)
Plaster of Paris, warm beige
Height: 31⅛″; width: shoulders 24″, back to front 13″;
plinth: 1⅛″ × 11″ × 9⅜″
W. Tyler, 1888

PART FOUR

Twentieth Century

Cricket in the twentieth century got off to the best possible start. The players of the Golden Age paraded their talents on an ever-widening canvas as the game became truly international, and ever more fascinating to all strata of society.

The MCC took over responsibility for overseas tours in 1903 (previously the charge of individuals and sponsors) and the first such expedition under their control, Pelham Warner's 1903–4 team to Australia, regained their Ashes (see pages 138–9) that had been surrendered to the marvellous 1902 Australian side in England. The initial venture to South Africa under the MCC banner in 1905–6 was less successful, the South Africans winning their first ever Test series against England 4–1, having never won so much as even one game of the four previous rubbers, all of which had been in South Africa. Warner did not have a full-strength England side at his disposal, but none the less the shock outcome put South Africa firmly on the map. A triangular series of matches between England, Australia and South Africa was played in England in 1912, a contest unfortunately all but ruined by appalling weather.

The First World War rudely interrupted organized cricket for the first time in its history. No first-class matches were played for four summers and, as if to fuel the pessimism of those who felt the game would never recover its former stature in a post-war era, both W. G. and Victor Trumper (the latter at the age of thirty-seven) died in 1915. But of course the game did survive, and remarkably few changes to its structure took place in the period between the wars. Expansion continued. By the outbreak of the Second World War, the Test-match fraternity had been extended to include the West Indies, New Zealand and India.

The mantle of the world's leading player passed from W. G. Grace to Jack Hobbs, and thence to a young man from Bowral, New South Wales, named Don Bradman. 'The Don' first came to England in 1930, aged twenty-one, after some prodigious batting feats in Australia, and continued to set statistical standards of batsmanship throughout his long career that are unlikely to be equalled. As player, captain and, in retirement, administrator, he dominated the scene as had no other cricketer bar Grace. The only threat to his infallibility came in 1932–3, during the infamous 'Bodyline' series in which D. R. Jardine, armed with the fearsome speed of Harold Larwood and Bill Voce, reduced Bradman's batting average to a mere 56, and nearly the Empire by one nation, so strained did Anglo-Australian relations become at one time. Bradman's greatest rivals were the masterly Gloucestershire batsman (and excellent bowler and outstanding slip-fielder) Walter Hammond, whose scores in Australia in 1928–9 were Bradmanesque before Bradman; and in later years the two greatest English batsmen whose careers straddled the Second World War, Len Hutton and Denis Compton.

For three or four seasons after 1945, the crowds flocked to County Championship and Test cricket just as they had done in the twenties and thirties, with the summer of 1947 the pinnacle. In that hot summer Denis Compton and Bill Edrich of Middlesex and England carried all before them, mainly at Lord's, in a glorious, apparently endless spree of run-making before enormous crowds that convinced most observers that the appeal of the game as it then stood was imperishable.

In fact, this proved not to be the case. As leisure time increased and rival attractions to fill that time proliferated in the fifties and sixties, cricket found it hard to hold on to its crowds and to compete in the commercial marketplace. Gradually, and sometimes painfully, the game changed with the times. The distinction between amateur and professional disappeared after the 1962 season; in 1963 the first one-day competition, the Gillette Cup, was introduced, and sponsorship became a life-line. One-day internationals followed the huge success of the shortened game at county level. The MCC relinquished its control of first-class cricket. From 1969 the private club no longer administered every aspect of the professional game but operated as one of three bodies that constituted the Cricket Council, the others being the Test and County Cricket Board and the National Cricket Association.

The Kerry Packer revolution of 1977, in which very many of the world's leading players deserted official Test cricket to play in an Australian television tycoon's independent commercial international competition, led to a drastic reappraisal of the professional's worth, and also to innovations such as floodlit night cricket. The stars of the seventies and eighties became high-profile personalities away from the cricket fields, sometimes with embarrassing consequences.

72

SMITH, Sir C. Aubrey
(1863–1948)
Drawing
13″ × 10½″
John Gilroy, 1948

Charles Aubrey Smith was educated at Charterhouse and at Cambridge, where he won a Blue all four years he was up. A fast-medium bowler, he made his debut for Sussex in 1882, was captain in 1887 and 1888, and played for the county until 1896. He toured Australia and captained the first English team to play in South Africa (1888–9), where he played his only Test.

Although his first-class cricket was played in the nineteenth century, he cannot be considered anything but a twentieth-century man. He was an accomplished actor and between the wars appeared in many Hollywood films. He did all he could to promote cricket in California and was knighted in 1944 in recognition of his efforts to further Anglo-American friendship.

John Gilroy was a landscape, figure and portrait painter who exhibited between 1927 and 1940. He donated the drawing to Lord's in 1955.

─── 73 ───
RANJITSINHJI, Kumar Shri
(HH Jam Sahib of Nawanagar)
(1872–1933)
A. Chevallier Tayler
28⅛″ × 14⅛″

─── 74 ───
RHODES, Wilfred
(1877–1973)
A. Chevallier Tayler
28⅛″ × 14⅛″

─── 75 ───
TYLDESLEY, John Thomas
(1873–1930)
A. Chevallier Tayler
28⅛″ × 14⅛″

These drawings were executed by
Chevallier Tayler (see page 41) in
1905. The four men depicted here
were all at the height of their
powers around the turn of the
century. In the case of Rhodes, in
particular, the skills and the career
were to march long into the 1900s.

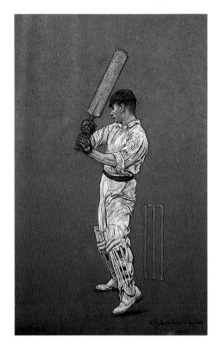

— 76 —

TROT, Albert Edwin
(1873–1914)
A. Chevallier Tayler
28⅛″ × 14⅛″

K. S. Ranjitsinhji (from 1907 His Highness the Jam Sahib of Nawanagar), educated at Rajkumar College in India, arrived at Cambridge University in 1893. He won a Blue but really only announced himself as a cricketer out of the ordinary when he scored 77 not out and 150 at Lord's in his first match for Sussex. From 1895 until 1904 he was the most prolific and exciting batsman in England. Several of Grace's outstanding records fell to him during this sensational phase of what was to be a long and glamorous career. In 1901 he made his highest score, 285 not out against Somerset, after having been up all night fishing. He played fifteen times for England from 1896 and toured both Australia and North America. He captained his adopted county from 1899 to 1903.

His technique was breathtaking – even in defence his bat became a weapon of exotic aggression. On inheriting his title in 1907 he was unable to devote as much time to cricket in England, but he played for Sussex as late as 1920 and graced the crease enough times to amass 72 centuries and the best part of 25,000 runs. He was a delegate to the League of Nations after the First World War.

Wilfred Rhodes has an all-round record which stands comparison even with that of W. G. Grace. The great Yorkshire slow left-arm bowler is the only man in first-class cricket to have captured more than 4000 wickets, on top of which he scored nearly 40,000 runs, a total surpassed by only fifteen other batsmen. He took 100 wickets in a season 23 times, seven times more than anyone else. He scored 1000 runs in a season 20 times, and in sixteen summers he achieved the 'double' of 1000 runs and 100 wickets, the latter feat unlikely ever to be approached.

Rhodes, a professional, was part of a long line of great Yorkshire left-armers; he took the place of Peel in the side in 1898, taking six wickets in his first game, and finishing his first season second in the national bowling averages with 154 wickets. He played first for England in 1899, and finally on the 1929–30 tour of the West Indies; although the best-remembered moment of his later playing years is his return to the England team in the final Australian match of 1926 when his bowling at the age of forty-nine played a decisive part in England's winning of the Ashes for the first time since before the First World War. He lived to be ninety-five and followed cricket with keen interest right until the very end, despite blindness in his old age.

J. T. Tyldesley, the Lancashire and England number three batsman, was, at his peak, England's leading professional batsman. His career figures, good as they are, and particularly his Test-match figures, do not do justice to his skills and temperament in difficult circumstances. He first appeared for Lancashire in 1895 and took only two matches to establish himself in the side, for whom he played his last game in 1923. He toured Australia twice and South Africa once, playing in all 31 times for England. He was at his quick-footed best against fast bowling, but also showed rare skill in dealing with the South African googly attack of 1907. He played on after the war, even though closer to fifty than to forty, scoring 272 against Derbyshire in 1919. After retiring he became coach at Old Trafford until 1929.

A. E. Trott enjoyed a distinguished, if erratic all-round career for teams both in his native Australia and in England, but is best remembered for unusual facts and feats that cropped up from time to time during his playing days. For example, he played for both England and Australia, and in his benefit match (he was a Middlesex professional) in 1907 took four wickets in four balls and did the hat-trick later in the same innings. Above all, perhaps, he became the first (and to date, only) man to strike a ball over the current Lord's Pavilion (see page 113). Trott took his own life in 1914 after a long illness.

77

RHODES, Wilfred
(1877–1973)
Cricket ball,
9⅛″ circumference, 6oz
Manufacturers: Gunn & Moore

1903

78

RHODES, Wilfred
(1877–1973)
Cricket bat, 32″ long, 4¼″ wide,
2 lb 6 oz
Manufacturers: Gunn & Moore

1912

Two of Rhodes' finest hours are
represented here: his 15 wickets
for 124 against Australia at
Melbourne in 1903–4 by the ball,
and his part in what is still the
highest first-wicket partnership
ever made in Australia, 323 with
Hobbs in 1911–12, by the bat.

79

TROTT, Albert Edwin
(1873–1914)
Cricket bat, 34½″ long,
blade 22″, 2lb 5oz
Maker: Cobbett, St Marylebone,
c. 1899

This is the bat with which Trott struck his huge blow at Lord's (see page 111). He was playing against the Australians for the MCC and Ground on 31 July 1899; the bowler was one of his former countrymen, M. A. Noble. The ball hit one of the Pavilion chimney pots and disappeared behind the building. It was retrieved from the garden of No. 6 Grove End Road.

With these gloves G. L. Jessop faced the might of the 1902 Australian attack which included Trumble, Noble and Saunders. The summer was a wet one and the undoubted star of the Australian team was Victor Trumper. The visitors won the five-match series 2-1, but both of the last two games were sensationally close finishes, Australia winning at Old Trafford by 3 runs and England by one wicket at The Oval. Jessop played a famous part in The Oval victory by means of a magnificent innings of 104 in just 77 minutes.

He was the most consistently fast scoring batsman in cricket history; known as the 'Croucher' because of his stance at the wicket, he hardly ever let bowlers dictate to him. He made many very big innings in almost unbelievably short times, and although his unbridled aggression from ball one sometimes meant an early end to his innings, he scored over 1000 runs in 14 different seasons, playing for Cambridge (four Blues in four years 1896–9), Gloucestershire, London County and England (18 times) from 1894 to 1914 with the same brilliant fervour. As a fielder in the covers he was scarcely less spectacular, and he was also a distinguished fast bowler.

80

JESSOP, Gilbert Laird
(1874–1955)
Batting gloves, 30″ unstretched, 1902

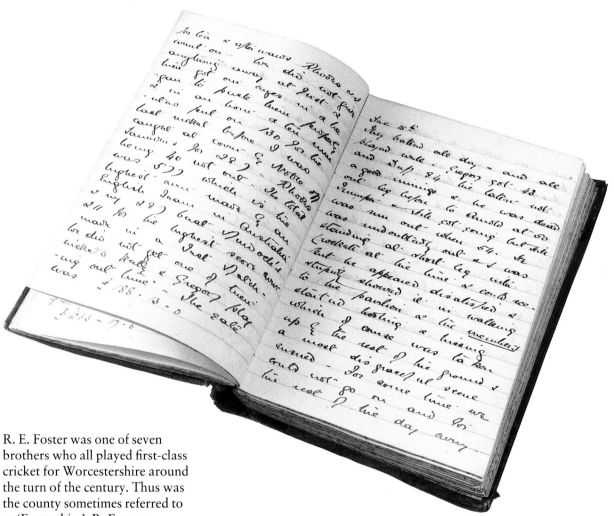

R. E. Foster was one of seven brothers who all played first-class cricket for Worcestershire around the turn of the century. Thus was the county sometimes referred to as 'Fostershire'. R. E. was a brilliant middle-order, right-hand batsman and a right-arm fast bowler. He won a cricket blue for four consecutive years at Oxford (1897–1900) and played 80 times for Worcestershire between 1899 and 1912. An amateur, he was unable to devote as much time as he would have wished to first-class cricket and only played one full season, that of 1901, when he scored 2128 runs at an average of over 50. He played eight times for England, and his greatest innings came in the First Test of the 1903–4 tour to Australia. He scored no less than 287 not out, at that time the highest individual score made by any player of either side in the history of Anglo-Australian Test Matches. It was not exceeded until Bradman scored 334 in 1930. He also represented his country at football. Foster died young, of diabetes.

In his personal account of the 1903–4 tour Foster describes the day he made his 287 not out.

81

FOSTER, Reginald Erskine
(1878–1914)
Diary, 8″ × 5″, 1903–4

The only known portrait of one of England's greatest ever all-round athletes, C. B. Fry, this was painted when its subject was nearly eighty, his vitality shining through the years. Fry was a brilliant sportsman: a triple Blue at Oxford (cricket, athletics, soccer), holder of the world long-jump record for 21 years, a member of the Southampton 1902 Cup Final team, an England soccer international and, of course, one of the most distinguished cricketers of his time. He played 26 times for England from 1895–6 to 1912, captaining the undefeated side in the Triangular tournament of the last-named year. A superb batsman, both as opener and in the middle order, he scored over 30,000 runs in his career at an average of over 50, primarily for Sussex, Hampshire, the Gentlemen and England. Six times he topped the season's batting averages, his greatest year being 1901 when he scored six centuries in successive innings and totalled 3147 runs.

He was an accomplished classicist and writer, stood unsuccessfully for Parliament several times and acted as India's representative at the League of Nations after the First World War. He never toured Australia as a cricketer, declining more than one invitation to do so. Fry is celebrated for having refused the throne of Albania. In his autobiography *Life Worth Living* (1939) he writes:

I do not say that I received a specific and definite invitation to become King of Albania, but in the indirect manner which so often characterises any affair in which an eminent Indian is

concerned it amounts to this – I was well in the running for the billet.

The eminent Indian referred to is Ranjitsinhji. Both he and Fry were League of Nations representatives, and partners and friends in politics as well as for Sussex and England at cricket.

Edmund Nelson (1910–   ) is a contemporary painter whose work includes portraits of G. M. Trevelyan and E. M. Forster, both displayed in halls at Cambridge.

82

FRY, Charles Burgess
Oil on canvas 32″ × 29″
Edmund Nelson, *c.* 1950

F. S. Jackson was an outstanding all-rounder of the Golden Age. He played for Harrow, Cambridge (a Blue every year from 1890 to 1893), Yorkshire (1890–1907) and England (twenty Tests 1893–1905). His greatest year was 1905 when he captained England against Australia. He won all five tosses, made more runs than any player on either side, at the highest average, and also topped the bowling averages. England won the series 2–0.

He saw active service in the Boer War, was MP for Howdenshire 1915–26 and Chairman of the Unionist Party in 1923, and was later Governor of Bengal. He was President of the MCC in 1921.

83

JACKSON, the Hon. Sir Francis
Stanley
(1870–1947)
Oil on canvas 28″ × 25″
English school, date unknown

This large picture of Sydney Barnes was painted when the great bowler was over eighty.

Sydney Barnes has as good a claim as any other bowler to be regarded as the greatest in all cricketing history, even though many men have far exceeded his tally of 719 first-class wickets. He was born in Staffordshire and it was for that Minor (in cricket terms) County and for teams in northern leagues that he played most of his cricket. There he captured a huge number of wickets: over 1400 at just 8 runs each for Staffordshire, and nearly 4000 at less than 7 runs apiece in the leagues. He was still taking wickets at remarkably low cost during his last season, 1934, when he was sixty-one years old.

He ventured into first-class cricket with both Warwickshire (1894–6) and Lancashire (1899–1903) but never found the senior county circuit to his liking. He none the less played 27 times for England from 1901 to 1914, although only ten of these appearances were at home. A. C. MacLaren, his county captain (Lancashire), first picked Barnes for England as a member of his Australian party of 1901–2, but it was on his second trip there ten years later that he was seen at the summit of his powers. He took 34 wickets in England's triumphant 1911–12 series and followed immediately with another 34 wickets in the three matches against South Africa in England during the 1912 Triangular tournament. In the winter of 1913–14, again against South Africa, he topped all previous efforts by taking no less than 49 wickets in just four Tests, including the then record of 17 in one match. By then he was forty. His total of 189 Test wickets was not overtaken until he had lived for another forty years.

Barnes mastered all subtleties of flight, swing and length; he could turn the ball with equal facility to the off or to the leg at fast-medium or slow-medium pace, and could also bowl all day if required. His disciplined, long-fingered menace is certainly evident in this portrait.

84

BARNES, Sydney Francis
(1873–1967)
Oil on canvas 49¾″ × 40″
H. Rutherford, 1954

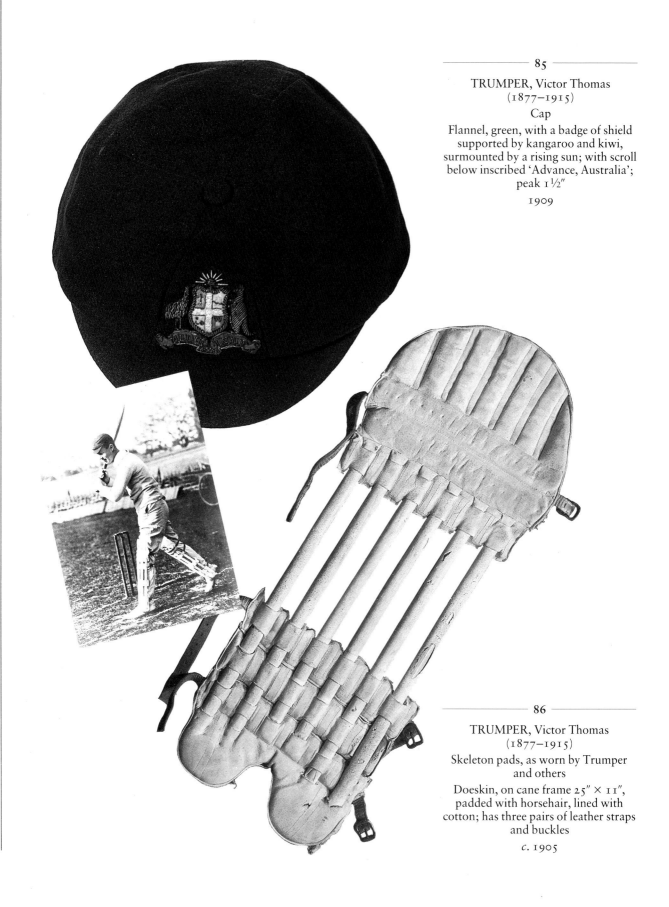

85

TRUMPER, Victor Thomas
(1877–1915)
Cap
Flannel, green, with a badge of shield
supported by kangaroo and kiwi,
surmounted by a rising sun; with scroll
below inscribed 'Advance, Australia';
peak 1½"
1909

86

TRUMPER, Victor Thomas
(1877–1915)
Skeleton pads, as worn by Trumper
and others
Doeskin, on cane frame 25" × 11",
padded with horsehair, lined with
cotton; has three pairs of leather straps
and buckles
c. 1905

87

TRUMPER, Victor Thomas
(1877–1915)

Bat

Probably that used by Trumper on the
1905 tour to England

34¼″ high, 22″ blade

Maker: Crawford, *c*. 1905

Inscription, written by Trumper,
reads: 'This which I selected at the
beginning of our tour is the best I have
ever used and never want a better –
V. Trumper'

Victor Trumper's contemporaries
at the turn of the century
considered him the greatest
batsman of their day, and almost
certainly the greatest ever. Even the
incredible feats of Bradman two
decades after Trumper's death
failed to change the view of many
that 'there'll never be another
Victor'.

Figures do not appear to justify
this claim, but Trumper was a man
who usually felt one hundred was
enough. He toured England four
times, but only in 1902, when he
scored eleven hundreds and 2570
runs in a wet summer, was his
progress there triumphant. It was
the manner of his scoring that
excited the superlatives. He raised
the art of batsmanship to a new
level; his strokes seemed instinctive
rather than planned, his reactions
quicksilver, his balance and timing
perfect. The greater the challenge
in terms of bowler or pitch, the
more likely was his genius to make
itself apparent.

He played for New South Wales
from 1894 to 1914 and for
Australia 48 times from 1899 to
1912. He died at the age of
thirty-seven from Bright's disease,
greatly mourned, four months
before the death of England's
champion, W. G. Grace. But Grace
had lived a life of normal span.

88

HOBBS, Sir John Berry
(1882–1963)

Cricket bat

Manufacturer: Summers, Brown and
Sons Ltd; 33⅜″ long, 22″ blade,
2 lb 6 oz

c. 1930

'Jack' Hobbs is universally
considered to have been England's
greatest-ever batsman. During his
long career, from 1905 to 1934, he
opened the batting for Surrey and
England with consistent and
outstanding success; no batsman
before or since has scored as many
runs or made as many hundreds. In
his first match for Surrey he scored
88 against a Gentlemen of England
side captained by W. G. Grace; his
final Test series in 1930 was Don
Bradman's first in England;
Hobbs' playing days were thus a
link between the eras of the game's
first Colossus and its third – with
Hobbs himself, of course, as the
second.

Of his 197 centuries, 98 were
made after his fortieth birthday;
his total aggregate of 61,237 runs
would have been higher still
without the intervention of the
First World War. He holds the
record for the highest individual
score made at Lord's – 316 not out
for Surrey against Middlesex in
1926. He formed famous opening
partnerships with three different
colleagues: Thomas Hayward and
then Andrew Sandham for Surrey,
and Herbert Sutcliffe for England.
Hobbs was an outstanding fielder
at cover and a useful right-arm
medium-pace bowler, and his
batsmanship on difficult wickets
led many to rate him the best of
any age. His modesty was as
remarkable as his success. He was
knighted in 1953.

Hobbs, a member of the
Maharaj Kumar of Vizianagram's
team in India and Ceylon in
1930–1, presented this bat to his
host in December 1930. The
Maharaj Kumar of Vizianagram in
turn presented the bat to the
President of the MCC in India
(G. O. Allen) during the 1963–4

tour. The inscription on the bat
reads:

To my dear friend the Maharaj Kumar
of Vizianagram from J. B. Hobbs, 21st
December 1930. I used this bat in my
last test match against Australia at the
Oval, August 1930, also while scoring
my first century in India at Benares,
November 1930.

The cigarette case was given to
Hobbs by the Maharaj Kumar's
wife, the Maharanee of
Vizianagram, also in 1930. It is
inscribed:

Keep this as a remembrance of your
visit to my house. My husband's
greatest hobby is cricket. My earnest
desire is that you should win for him

—— 89 ——
HOBBS, Sir John Berry
(1882–1963)
Silver cigarette case
4″ high, 3″ wide, ¼″ deep

all the matches. Our XI should be
looked upon as the invincibles.

Vizianagram (1905–65) was a
great patron of Indian cricket and
captained the 1936 Indian team to
England, playing in all three Tests.
During the tour he was knighted.
He was President of the Indian
Cricket Board of Control from
1954 to 1956 and was also an
Indian MP.

Frank Woolley, one of the game's greatest all-round players, delighted cricket-lovers for the best part of a third of a century with his graceful, unhurried yet quick-scoring left-handed batting and his medium to slow left-arm bowling. In addition he was a brilliant slip-fielder who still holds the record for the number of catches taken by a fielder in a career (1018).

Kent and England were the principal beneficiaries of his skills; he first played for his county in 1906 (he was born in Tonbridge) and for his country in 1909. He scored 1000 runs in 28 separate seasons, his best being 1928 when he put together 3352. His highest score was 305 in and against Tasmania, for the MCC in 1911–12. Only Hobbs finished playing with more runs to his name than Woolley's final total of 58,959.

As a bowler his finest year was 1920, when he took 185 wickets, although in seven other summers he captured 100 victims or more. In all he achieved the 'double' eight times. He retired with 2066 wickets to his name.

Sculptor *Wilhelm Soukop* (1907–   ) arrived in England in 1934 after education and apprenticeship with an engraver in Vienna. He has executed many sculptures for both public and private institutions and individuals, has taught extensively in England, and became a Royal Academician in 1969.

90

WOOLLEY, Frank Edward
(1887–1978)
Bust, cast bronze, 16″ high
Wilhelm Soukop RA, *c.* 1960

BRADMAN, Sir Donald George
(1908–   )
Oil on canvas 40″ × 35″
R. Hannaford, 1972

The only cricketer whose celebrity
during his playing days challenged
that of W. G. Grace during his is
Don Bradman, the 'boy from
Bowral', New South Wales. He
was born in Cootamundra, NSW,
but was brought up in Bowral,
eighty miles from Sydney. He is
quite simply the greatest
run-maker the game has ever seen.

He burst into first-class cricket
in 1927 with a century in his first
match for New South Wales, and
from then until his retirement in
1948–9 he maintained a quite
stupendous record of achievement
that no other batsman has
approached. There will always be
arguments about who was
technically or stylistically the
greatest batsman of all time –
Trumper? Hobbs? Bradman? – but
there can be no dispute about the
most effective. Bradman's career
average of 95.14 is so far ahead of
the field, as is his overall test
average of 99.94, that supporters
of rival champions are unwise to
use figures as evidence.

He never lost a rubber as captain
of Australia, including four series
against England. He was knighted
in 1949. He continued to make a
major contribution to the game
after retirement, as a writer,
selector and Chairman of the
Australian Board of Control.

The painting by R. Hannaford was
sponsored by the Commercial
Bank of Australia.

BRADMAN, Sir Donald George
(1908–   )
Boots 11¼″ × 7″
Technic, c. 1947

Bradman wore this trusty pair of
boots towards the end of his
career.

This portrait of one of England's most famous captains was painted just a year after the 'Bodyline' tour in which Jardine ruthlessly led England to a 4–1 victory in a series that was almost called off half-way through. The leg-theory tactics that Jardine had employed to keep the phenomenal Don Bradman's scores down to almost acceptable levels, via his fast bowlers Larwood and Voce, came near to causing a complete breakdown in Anglo-Australian relations, and not just cricketing relations.

Jardine (Oxford University and Surrey) played twenty-two times for England, leading his country in fifteen, losing only once. He scored almost 15,000 runs in his career, at an average of nearly 47 – extremely impressive figures for which he is, however, hardly ever remembered, thanks to the notoriety of his captaincy during that infamous tour.

93

JARDINE, Douglas Robert
(1900–1958)
Oil on canvas 35½″ × 30¾″
Herbert A. Olivier, 1934

The blazer worn by G. O. B. Allen, as he then was, on the Jardine 'Bodyline' tour of 1932–3. (See also page 125).

94

ALLEN, Sir George Oswald Browning
(1902–   )
Blazer, 33½″ long, 25″ sleeve
1932

This was the bat with which Len Hutton, at the age of 22, played perhaps the most famous innings in the history of cricket – his mighty 364 against Australia at Kennington Oval, in August 1938. This was the highest individual score by a batsman in international cricket and remained so for twenty years. It was the principal contribution to the highest score ever compiled by a team in one innings of a Test match – 903 for 7 declared.

Even before this astounding feat, which for once put Don Bradman into the shade, Len Hutton had shown himself to be a player out of the ordinary, a worthy successor to Herbert Sutcliffe as opening batsman for both Yorkshire and England. His career was of course interrupted by the Second World War, denying him six seasons when he would have been at his very best. It was during the war that he sustained a serious injury to his left arm, leaving it slightly shorter than his right. However he overcame this difficulty to take up his position as England's leading batsman in the decade from 1945, with only Denis Compton, in a completely different fashion, challenging his supremacy during that time.

In 1952 Hutton was appointed captain of England, the first professional cricketer to be thus honoured. He led England to sweeping success that year against a weak Indian side. The following year he achieved an infinitely more satisfying victory when he led England to their first post-war Ashes triumph. A difficult series in the West Indies in the winter of 1953–4 was drawn with Hutton's batting and captaincy crucial throughout. He missed a great deal of the gloomy 1954 summer through injury but returned in glory to the full-time Test arena when he retained the Ashes for his country Down Under in 1954–5. This was a gripping series in which Hutton's faith in the fast bowling of Tyson and Statham played such an important part. He was appointed to lead England in the 1955 series against South Africa but he was not fit enough to do so. He retired from regular first-class cricket at the end of the 1955 season.

His wonderful career figures of more than 40,000 runs and 129 centuries are a fitting tribute to his batsmanship, as was the knighthood he received in 1956 to his qualities of leadership and unassuming manner; only a truly great sportsman could have lived up to the fame his 364 from this bat brought him – Hutton did so.

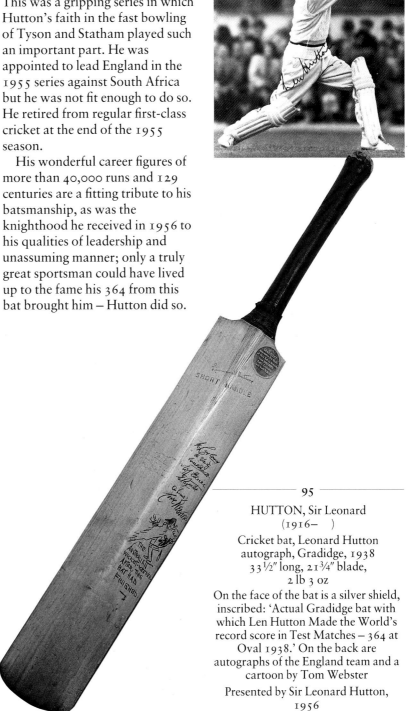

95

HUTTON, Sir Leonard
(1916–   )
Cricket bat, Leonard Hutton autograph, Gradidge, 1938
33½″ long, 21¾″ blade,
2 lb 3 oz
On the face of the bat is a silver shield, inscribed: 'Actual Gradidge bat with which Len Hutton Made the World's record score in Test Matches – 364 at Oval 1938.' On the back are autographs of the England team and a cartoon by Tom Webster

Presented by Sir Leonard Hutton, 1956

Just as Len Hutton was held to represent the solid, sometimes uncompromising side of English batsmanship, so Denis Compton, his only rival as the premier English batsman in the ten years after the Second World War, was portrayed as a carefree genius. Both views are over-simplifications but they are not inaccurate. Compton's attitude and approach to the game never seemed as serious or as world-weary as Hutton's. Because of this, his career underwent some dramatic ups and downs, none more up than the summer of 1947.

In that long, hot season Compton and his Middlesex and England colleague W. J. Edrich carried all before them. Both scored more runs in one English season than any other batsman has before or since. Compton's incredible final tally was 3816, Edrich's 3539. They filled grounds all over the country, whether playing for England against South Africa or for Middlesex in a county championship game. Cricket seemed to be as popular that summer with the paying public as it had ever been in its history. Compton was the perfect hero for a nation still finding its feet after the war, still deprived of a wide choice of entertainment, still making up for the six summers without any first-class cricket at all. He was handsome, talented and charming; apparently effortlessly successful.

Like Hutton's, Compton's career had just got into its stride before the war. He first appeared for Middlesex, batting at number eleven, in 1936, but was soon moved well up the order. He had established himself in the England side by 1939 (he scored just 1 run in the match in which Hutton made his 364). The late forties were his great years, with 1947 the best of them all. A soccer injury to his knee began to cause him serious problems by the early fifties, but other than on one terrible tour to Australia in 1950–1, when he was unable to find any form at all during the Test Matches, his marvellous natural ability still enabled him to play many outstanding innings. Many of his improvised shots that brought him a hefty percentage of his almost 39,000 runs have still to reach the text books.

96

COMPTON, Denis Charles Scott, CBE
(1918–   )
Cricket bat, Warsop, *c.* 1947
34″ long, 22″ blade,
2 lb 4 oz
Inscription on face: 'With this bat I scored 3816 runs including 18 centuries [in] 1947. Sincerely yours, Denis Compton'
Presented by Benjamin Warsop and Denis Compton, 1956

This huge and striking portrait of one of England's most famous fast bowlers was painted by Spear when 'Fiery Fred' was still opening England's attack eleven years after his explosive Test debut.

In 1952 a young Trueman tore through the fragile batting of the Indian Test side, taking 29 wickets for England in the four-match series. However, he was to find progress to lasting prominence at the top level difficult. The outspoken Yorkshireman was not always looked upon with great favour by the authorities and missed selection for several Tests to which his undoubted ability entitled him. When two other great fast bowlers of the era, Frank Tyson and Brian Statham, bowled so superbly in Australia in 1954–5, a tour for which he was not chosen, even the self-confident Trueman must have wondered whether he had a Test future.

By the end of the fifties, however, all had been forgiven and Trueman was an essential part of England's opening attack, and established as one of the game's best-loved personalities. In 1964 he became the first bowler to take 300 Test wickets. After his retirement in 1969 (though he played some one-day games for Derbyshire in 1972) he became a broadcaster and writer on the game, thus enabling those generations not fortunate enough to have witnessed him in full flow on the field to appreciate his down-to-earth approach to the game.

Ruskin Spear (1911–) is well known for the boldness of his portraits; Trueman's personality is well suited to his aggressively colourful style. He first exhibited at the Royal Academy in 1932. This picture is on extended loan to MCC from the Lord's Taverners.

97
TRUEMAN, Frederick Sewards
(1931–)
Oil on canvas 82″ × 26½″
Ruskin Spear CBE, 1963

No doubt sculptor David Wynne and the man who commissioned this work, Lord Rosebery (who presented it to the MCC in 1954), were inspired to create a figure of England's first great post-Second World War bowler by Bedser's superb performances during the England–Australia series of Coronation year, in which the Surrey medium-fast bowler took a then record 39 wickets, a major factor in England's recapture of the Ashes after a long period of failure against the old enemy.

Few men have served cricket as well as Alec Bedser. He and his identical twin brother Eric first played for Surrey in 1939, but the war deprived them of six seasons of first-class cricket before they became established members of the side. It was quickly apparent in 1946 that not only Surrey but England had an outstanding opening bowler in Alec Bedser. For some time after the war he lacked any support of stature in a not very successful England side, but nevertheless in match after match he returned outstanding figures. He took eleven wickets in each of his first two Tests, against India, and 30 wickets in the 1950–1 Australian series. His performances in 1953 surpassed even this mighty effort, with his 14 for 99 in the First Test at Trent Bridge paramount. Bradman rated him the best English bowler he played against. He was a vital part of Surrey's seven-in-a-row Championship side of the fifties. In 1962 he became a selector, becoming Chairman in 1969, a post he held until 1981.

David Wynne (1926–   ) had no formal artistic training but after a naval career in the war turned to sculpture with great success. He

first exhibited in 1950 and since then has executed a wide body of work all over the world. His many large works are to be seen in churches, cathedrals, hotels and other public places in several cities in Britain and across America. His bronze portraits include The Queen, the Prince of Wales, the Beatles, Pelé and Shergar.

98

BEDSER, Alec Victor, OBE
(1918–   )
Bronze figure, mounted on green and black marble pedestal and plinth
27½″ high overall
David Wynne, 1953

The most famous bowling feat in international cricket, if not in all cricket, is Jim Laker's nineteen wickets for 90 runs for England against Australia in the Fourth Test at Old Trafford, Manchester in 1956. With the two balls displayed here, the Yorkshire-born Laker took nine Australian wickets for 37 in the first innings and all ten for 53 in the second. No one before or since has taken more than seventeen wickets in one game, nor ten in one innings in a Test. Almost incidentally, England won the match and retained the Ashes.

Laker was an outstanding off-break bowler who bowled with great distinction for Surrey from 1946 to 1959, and for England in 46 Tests between 1947 and 1959. After retirement, he embarked upon a second successful career in cricket, as a television commentator.

99

LAKER, James Charles
(1922–1986)
Two cricket balls,
9″ circumference
Manufacturer: Stuart Surridge, 1956

On 5 July 1973, on the second day of the Kent *v* Surrey match at Maidstone, Colin Cowdrey, batting at number seven, scored the 100th hundred of his first-class career. This plate, listing details of every one of the centuries, was issued to commemorate the achievement. The first Century of Centuries dinner plate was the 1896 tribute to W. G. Grace, who had reached the rare target the previous summer (see page 104).

Cowdrey first appeared at Lord's at the age of thirteen – the youngest player ever to play there in an important match – when he represented Tonbridge School. His first-class career for Kent began in 1950 and he also played for Oxford from 1952 to 1954. The first of his record 114 Tests for England was in 1954–5 when he and Peter May emerged as the leaders of a new generation of post-war batsmen. Cowdrey captained England no fewer than 27 times, but his main chance to

100

COWDREY, Michael Colin
(1932–)
Century of Centuries dinner plate
9″ diameter
Manufacturer: Coalport
1973

establish a secure hold on the highest honour in English cricket was frustrated through injury in 1969. He scored over 42,000 runs in his career, with a final tally of 107 centuries.

With these gloves Bob Taylor of Derbyshire and England in 1985 made his 1528th dismissal in first-class cricket, thus beating the world record, until then held by John Murray of Middlesex and England.

Taylor made his debut for Derbyshire in 1963 and soon established himself as one of the world's best wicket-keepers. He was none the less unfortunate as far as international opportunities were concerned in that his career coincided with that of another genius of the gauntlets, Alan Knott of Kent. All the same he played 51 times for England and came out of retirement for a couple of hours during the England–New Zealand Test at Lord's in 1986 when Bruce French was injured. The remains of the interrupted lunch he was eating that day have not been preserved in the Lord's Museum.

—— 101 ——
TAYLOR, Robert William
(1941–)
Wicket-keeping gloves 11¼″ × 7″
Manufacturer: Mitre
1985

The twentieth-century cricketing landscape has perhaps not been served as well by artists as were the previous two centuries, but of course the efforts of the modern artist are more likely to grow in appeal as time goes by. Two pictures that are indisputably holding their own against the competition of their elders are paintings by Arthur Mailey, probably the most gifted cricketing artist since Felix, and by Lawrence Toynbee.

A. A. Mailey (1886–1967) was a
fine leg-break and googly bowler
who played for New South Wales
from 1912 to 1930 and 21 times
for Australia in the 1920s. And he
was just as adept with the pen and
brush as he was with the ball. He
painted or drew many cricketing
subjects during his lifetime,
including cartoon caricatures of his
cricketing contemporaries and
studies of grounds, such as this
beautiful painting of what is
reputed to be the smallest cricket
ground in the world, the 'Valley of
Peace', Christchurch, New
Zealand.

He was also a fine writer and
journalist, whose entertaining
autobiography, published in 1958,
was entitled *10 for 66 and All
That*, inspired by the occasion in
1921 when, playing for the
Australians, he took all ten
Gloucestershire wickets in one
innings. He, rather unfairly, holds
the record for the most runs
conceded by one bowler in one
innings – 362 (he took four
wickets) when Victoria amassed
the staggering total of 1107 against
New South Wales at Melbourne in
1926–7. Mailey always claimed
that his figures would have been

102

THE VALLEY OF PEACE,
Christchurch, New Zealand
Oil on canvas 14″ × 19″
Arthur Mailey *c.* 1961

better but for a chap in the
grandstand dropping several
catches.

A gentle interpretation of a game in progress at Oxford University's lovely ground, where admission is still free. The University has played there since 1881.

Lawrence Toynbee (1922–   ) studied at the Ruskin School of Drawing, Oxford. He is the son of Arnold Toynbee the historian and the grandson of Gilbert Murray, the celebrated classical scholar. Now based in York, he is represented at Lord's by 'Cricket in the Parks' and also by 'Hit to Leg'.

— 103 —
CRICKET IN THE PARKS, OXFORD
Oil on canvas 16½″ × 23″
Lawrence Toynbee, 1953

PART FIVE

Curiouser and Curiouser

Lord's is home to many unusual trophies and objects, some of which have minimal intrinsic value – all of which are of maximum fascination to the cricket-lover. Foremost among these is, of course, the game's most celebrated prize – the Ashes, played for at approximately two-yearly intervals by England and Australia. A selection of the peculiar follows.

———————— 104 ————————

THE ASHES
Urn

Height: 4³⁄₁₆″ (4¼″ with cork);
diameter of base: 1⅜″; width of
shoulder: 1⅝″

Pottery, dark red (presumably
Australian), containing the ashes of a
bail (probably), sealed by a cork

1883

The most famous trophy in cricket (if not all sport) is a tiny urn, in itself worth very little, containing the remains of burnt wood, worth even less. On 29 August 1882, at The Oval, Australia defeated the full strength of England on English soil in what remains one of the most dramatic Test matches ever played, by just 7 runs. The following day an 'obituary' notice appeared in the *Sporting Times*, written by Shirley Brooks, son of an editor of *Punch*, as follows:

In affectionate remembrance of English Cricket which died at The Oval, 29th August, 1882. Deeply lamented by a large circle of sorrowing friends and acquaintances, R.I.P. N.B. The body will be cremated and the ashes taken to Australia.

That winter the Hon. Ivo Bligh, later Lord Darnley, led a team Down Under to recover the mythical Ashes. Australia won the First Test, but England were victorious in the next two; consequently the real Ashes came into being when some Melbourne women burned a bail used in the third game and presented the ashes in an urn to Bligh.

That is the official story; some have claimed that as the Third Test was played at Sydney, the presentation took place earlier in the tour at Melbourne, that the contents are not the ashes of a bail but of a ball, and that Bligh never won them back anyway in 1882–3, as Australia won the fourth match, thus levelling the series 2–2.

However, in an interview in 1894 Bligh is quoted by W. A. Bettesworth thus:

Some verses were published in *Punch* to the effect that English cricket had been cremated at The Oval when Murdoch's team beat England and that 'St Ivo' was taking a team to bring back 'The Ashes'. When we had beaten Murdoch's team a second time a number of Australian ladies presented me with a pretty little urn containing ashes, which according to the title written on the urn were 'The Ashes of English Cricket'. We played Murdoch's Australian XI three Matches, winning two and losing one. A fourth match was arranged to give two other men a chance which ended in defeat.

One of those ladies at least was definitely from the state of Victoria, if not from Melbourne itself – Miss Florence Rose Morphy, of Beechwood. She married Bligh in 1884. After the death of her husband, who had become the 8th Earl Darnley in 1900, Lady Darnley presented the urn to the MCC.

A verse printed on a label attached to the urn reads as follows:

When Ivo goes back with the urn,
    the urn;
Studds, Steel, Read and Tylecote
    return, return;
The welkin will ring loud,
The great crowd will feel proud
Seeing Barlow and Bates with the
    urn, the urn;
And the rest coming home with
    the urn

The players mentioned were all members of Bligh's 1882–3 side. There were two brothers named Studd in the team, C. T. and G. B.

The other items in the case with the urn are a small bag for the urn, the gift of Mrs J. W. Fletcher of Brisbane; the design for the bag drawn by Mrs Fletcher; a letter from Bligh thanking Mrs Fletcher; the scorecard of the 1882 Oval Test and batting lists of the two teams for that match, autographed by the two captains, A. N. Hornby and W. L. Murdoch.

The Ashes never left Lord's, even when they were held by Australia, from the time of Lady Darnley's presentation until January 1988 when, at the request of the Australian Board of Control, a unique decision was taken by the MCC to allow the Ashes to be exhibited in Sydney during the England–Australia Test match held to commemorate the Bicentenary of Australia the nation.

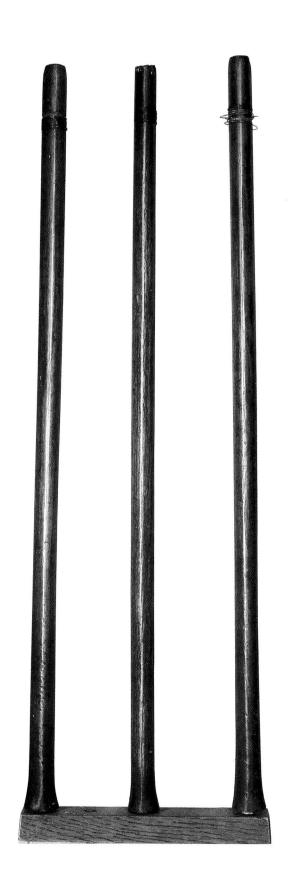

The oldest surviving wicket at Lord's was in use from 1798 until 1821. Wickets originally consisted of just two stumps, which meant of course that straight deliveries often failed to dislodge the bail, enabling the morally defeated batsman to stay in. Thanks to a Surrey player known as 'Lumpy' (real name Edward Stevens), the most feared bowler in the land in the 1770s, the third stump came into regular being. Such was his accuracy that he bowled right through John Small's wicket three times in an important match in 1775, but to no avail: the reprieved Small (playing for Hambledon) scraped the final runs needed for victory. The injustice of this result in particular soon led to the introduction of the middle peg.

There is a model of a two-stump wicket in the Memorial Gallery, but no original version.

——— 105 ———
Three-stump wicket, bails missing
24″ high
Fitted into a modern stand

Oak
1798

This extraordinary memento was presented by the Free Foresters Cricket Club, itself only seven years old at the time, to the Reverend William Bedford in March 1863. Bedford was the founder of the Free Foresters.

A ram and ewe loiter at the foot of a splayed oak tree. The tablet is engraved as follows:

In grateful memory of long services and tried friendship this token of esteem is presented to the Reverend W. K. R. Bedford, Rector of Sutton Coldfield and sometime Secretary of the Free Foresters by his most attached friends and affectionate brethren of the club – March 1863

Supported on the branches is a fluted bowl of inverted umbrella shape with serrated edge.

William Kirkpatrick Riland Bedford (1827–1905) was rector of Sutton Coldfield, near Birmingham, for over forty years. He founded the Free Foresters in 1856 and was the author of *The Annals of the Free Foresters*, published in 1895. He was also a recognized authority on boating and archery. Never a great cricketer on the field of play, he was a marvellous supporter of the game off it.

106

BEDFORD, The Reverend W. K. R.
Silver centrepiece stand
Silver and cut glass
Height: 19″; silver portion only 17″; diameter of base: 7⅜″; diameter of bowl: 10″; weight of silver: 90 oz
Elkington & Co., Birmingham, 1862
(Birmingham hallmark of 1862)

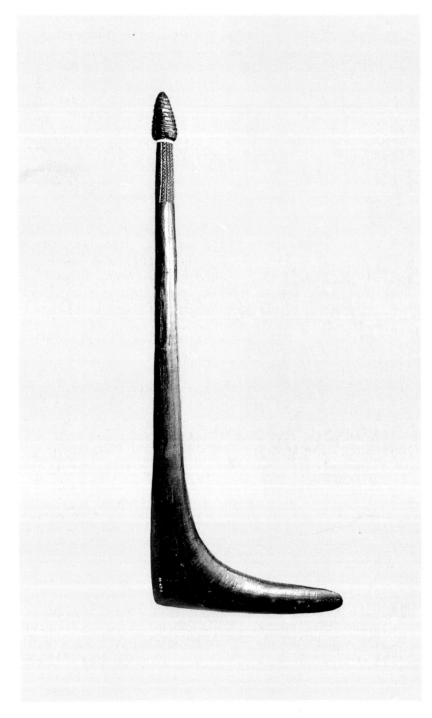

In 1868, the first tour of England by a cricket team from overseas took place. The team was Australian, but aboriginal. The side was captained by Charles Lawrence, the Surrey cricketer, who had stayed on in Australia after touring with the 1861 English team under H. H. Stephenson. Coached by T. W. Wills of Victoria, the Aborigines played 47 matches in England, winning fourteen, losing fourteen and drawing nineteen. At Lord's they lost to MCC but led on first innings with their star player, Johnny Mullagh, scoring 75.

The other colourfully named members of the side were King Cole (who, sad to say, contracted pneumonia during the trip and died in London), Tarpot, Dick-a-Dick, Jellico, Peter, Red Cap, Mosquito, Harry Rose, Bullocky and Cuzens.

After each match the Aborigines entertained the crowds with various of their native athletic skills including spear and boomerang throwing. The nulla-nulla or leowel is a war weapon. This particular one was used by Dick-a-Dick during the tour 'when defending himself against showers of cricket balls thrown at him at a few yards' distance', according to the attached label. At Lewisham, Dick-a-Dick's ball-dodging earned him £2 10s.

107

Nulla-nulla (leowel)
Wood, brown, polished, L-shaped
Length to heel: 27″; to toe: 10¾″
c. 1868

This unique trophy was presented to the Secretary of Surrey, Mr W. Burrup, for the part he played in helping to organize the first English tour of Australia, in 1861–2. The first overseas tour anywhere had been that undertaken by George Parr's side in 1859 to North America; this second venture was of far greater long-term significance for the future of international cricket.

The tour was sponsored by the Melbourne catering firm of Spiers and Pond after they had failed to secure Charles Dickens for a lecture tour. The great author had a fondness for cricket, but probably never realized that his reluctance to go Down Under was the greatest service he ever did the game.

Seven of the party, including the captain, Heathfield Harman Stephenson, came from Burrup's county. They left Liverpool on 20 October 1861 and arrived in Melbourne (via the Cape) on Christmas Eve. They lost only two matches, both against teams containing 22 players.

The inscription on the egg reads: 'S & P to W. B., Melbourne 1882' (i.e. Spiers and Pond to William Burrup).

William Burrup (1820–1901) and his twin brother John (1820–1900) were both stout servants of Surrey County Cricket Club in its formative years. Both were founder members of the club in 1845 and both were Honorary Secretary, John from 1848 to 1855, William from 1855 to 1872.

108

BURRUP, William
(1802–1901)
Emu's egg, 5″ high
c. 1861–2

Henry Fehr, a professional sculptor, was the uncle of the young boy whose stance in short trousers he immortalized in bronze. Rupert's life was tragically short. He was an indirect victim of the First World War in that he died after catching an illness from soldiers who were billeted in the Fehr family home. The statue was created posthumously from photographs and presented as a long-term loan by Rupert Fehr's sisters in 1971.

109

FEHR, Rupert James
(1908–16)
Bronze statuette
Height: 3′8″
Henry Fehr, *c.* 1917

Old Etonian Lord Harris (see pages 31–2) was sufficiently impressed by E. G. Whately's hat-trick in the 1900 Eton *v* Harrow match at Lord's to present the young bowler with this hat, inscribed with his bowling analysis of 24.3–8–59–5 and with the legend 'From Lord Harris to E. G. Whately Esq., Eton *v* Harrow 1900'.

Whately's efforts were not enough to win the game for Lord Harris's old school, however.

Harrow scraped home by one wicket after being set only 128 to win, Whately taking 5 for 59 in the innings (including his hat-trick) and 8 for 125 in the match.

Ellis George Whately, an off-break bowler, played just thirteen first-class games in his life, for Oxford University and Somerset. He did, however, take another hat-trick in 1903 – for Oxford University against the Gentlemen of Philadelphia.

— 110 —

E. G. WHATELY
(1882–1969)
Hat and ball
Glass and brass (the hat) 3½″ × 4¼″

THIS SPARROW WAS KILLED AT LORD'S BY A BALL
BOWLED BY JEHANGIR KHAN(CAMBRIDGE UNIVERSITY)
TO T. N. PEARCE (M. C. C.)
—— ON JULY 3ʳᵈ 1936. ——

Deaths on the cricket field are mercifully rare; even that of a bird is an unusual event, although over the years many feathered friends have ventured into fairly dangerous positions at crucial moments of play. One such was the unfortunate sparrow shown here, who intercepted a ball bowled by the Cambridge University bowler Jehangir Khan (father of Majid, and himself an Indian Test player) to T. N. Pearce, batting for the MCC at Lord's on 3 July 1936. Both ball and bird were declared dead. Jehangir Khan died in 1988.

III

Sparrow and ball
Height: 8½″ (with plinth); width: 11″
Manufacturer: Duke and Son
1936

The England and Australia players of the 1954–5 Ashes series are immortalized in an unusual way by cartoonist Tony Rafty on the surface of an Arthur Morris Slazenger bat. England, under Len Hutton, beat Ian Johnson's Australia 3–1, with fast bowlers Tyson and Statham their principal heroes.

The names on the bat are as follows:

D. C. S. Compton, L. Hutton, P. Loader, A. V. Bedser, T. G. Evans, J. B. Statham, J. H. Wardle, F. H. Tyson, R. T. Simpson, T. E. Bailey, J. V. Wilson, P. B. H. May, M. C. Cowdrey, K. V. Andrew, R. Appleyard, W. J. Edrich, T. W. Graveney, J. E. McConnon.

112

ENGLAND v. AUSTRALIA
1954–5
Bat 34¼″ long, 21¾″ blade
Slazengers, Arthur Morris autograph,
1954
Caricatures by Tony Rafty

This timepiece, which imitates a
typical grandfather clock but
without the front door, pendulum
or weights, has black Roman
numerals and a gilt rim. Its interest
to cricketers lies in the fact that its
body is carved from wood taken
from David Harris's cottage.
David Harris (see pages 74–5) was
the Hambledon Club's leading
bowler (right-hand, fast
under-arm). He played important
cricket until 1798 when gout
finally got the better of him.

On the plinth of the clock is a
metal plaque inscribed:

'David Harris (1755–1803) the great
Hambledon and England bowler. The
case of this clock is carved from a
beam taken from a cottage in
Crookham, Hampshire, occupied by
David Harris at the time of his death.
The clock was presented to Mr Claude
S. Buckingham by cricketers of
Crookham and neighbouring parishes
in 1911. It passed to MCC as a legacy
on Mr Buckingham's death in 1960.'

113

HARRIS, David
(1755–1803)
Miniature grandfather clock made
from beam in his cottage
Overall height: 27"; oak, dark brown

Few would have forecast when this ball was purchased that it would one day find its way to the Lord's Memorial Gallery, for its playing life began with a game at humble Cheetham Cricket Club. However, during the match it was hit over a 17-foot wall into the street where it struck Miss B. Stone. She successfully sued the club but the case went to the Court of Appeal where the decision was reversed. The House of Lords ultimately upheld the Court of Appeal's ruling.

114

THE NATIONAL CLUB CRICKET ASSOCIATION
Ball, 5½oz, on plinth with silver plate
Presented to the MCC by the NCCA, 1951
Made by T. Ives and Sons, Tonbridge

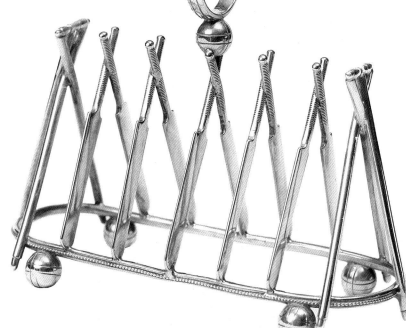

This delightful object consists of five crossed bats, with wickets at each end. The whole is surmounted by four balls and the central section is topped by a ball and buckle. MCC purchased the toast rack in 1971 from China Repairers of St John's Wood with whom they were doing some broken porcelain business at the time.

115

TOAST RACK
Silver gilt, 5¼″ high
Unknown designer, c. 1900

This was presented by the Kjobenhavns (Copenhagen) Boldklub to the MCC team that visited Denmark in 1952. Cricket has been played in that country since at least 1865; today there are some 40 clubs and 3000 players. The Danish national team achieved its first international victory, against Holland, in 1972. In 1979 Denmark participated in the ICC Trophy competition in England, obtaining four wins. MCC sides have toured Denmark frequently since the First World War.

—————— 116 ——————

KJOBENHAVNS BOLDKLUB
Royal Copenhagen Craquelee
porcelain bowl
2⅛″ high, 9⅞″ diameter, thickness of
rim 2⅛″

117

ROCHE, Emile
Silver christening mug, 1852
4″ high, 3¼″ diameter

The mug is adorned with cricketing scenes and was presented to the MCC by Mrs J. Taylerson, grand-daughter of Emile Roche, in 1968.

118

PARDON, Sydney Herbert
(1855–1925)
Silver match box, 1899
2½″ high, 1½″ wide, ¼″ deep

S. H. Pardon was the editor of *Wisden's Cricketers' Almanack* for 34 years. From 1891 until 1925 he produced the most important of all cricketing publications with 'loving care', as his successor C. Stewart Caine wrote in the 1926 edition. In addition to his great reputation as a cricket writer and critic, he followed music, drama and racing with zeal, writing professionally about all these subjects as well as about several other sports. His knowledge of plays and players, and of opera was encyclopaedic.

He is however best rememberd for his time at the helm at *Wisden*. This memento, depicting a kangaroo batting and a lion keeping wicket together with the slogan '*The Sportsman* for cricket news', was presented to him in 1899. The inscription reads as follows:

Souvenir of England v. Australia presented to S. H. Pardon by the proprietors of *The Sportsman*, London September 1899

The Melbourne Cricket Club, Australia's oldest existing cricket club, was formed in 1838, three years after the first settlement of the Port Phillip district. In 1853 the present Melbourne Cricket Ground, one of the world's most famous sporting centres, became the Club's ground. This Australian MCC has a collection of cricket art and memorabilia which rivals that of Lord's.

The inscription on the salver reads:

Presented to the Marylebone Cricket Club by the Melbourne Cricket Club to commemorate two notable milestones in the history of cricket, Melbourne 3 February 1988

Marylebone Cricket Club
200 years 1787–1987
Melbourne Cricket Club
150 years 1838–1988

119

MELBOURNE CRICKET CLUB
Silver salver with seven penguins on ice, 1987
2½″ high, 11″ × 11″ at base, diameter of dish 10¾″

This massive trophy is competed for by England and the world's youngest Test match nation, Sri Lanka. The first game between the two countries was played in Colombo in February 1982, the next two at Lord's in 1984 and 1988. England won the first and third of these matches and the 1984 Lord's game was drawn. Sri Lanka's progress in international cricket has been hampered by the country's internal political crises but no-one can doubt their right to full Test match status. Sri Lanka's first cricket club was formed in 1832 and English and MCC teams made regular visits to Ceylon, as it then was, from 1889.

The trophy is approximately one thousand times the volume of The Ashes!

The inscription on the trophy reads:

England Sri Lanka Cricket Tests Trophy
Awarded by His Excellency J. R. Jayawardena, President of the Democratic Socialist Republic of Sri Lanka, February 1982

120

ENGLAND v. SRI LANKA
Trophy, 36″ high, 23″ wide at top, diameter at base 12″

Acknowledgements

The author and publishers would like to thank the following for permission to reproduce the illustrations listed below:

Eton College for the Eton v Harrow scorebook 1805 (item no. 5)

Dennis Flanders for *The Long Room at Lord's 1953* (item no. 24)

North Yorkshire Record Office for a receipt for a member's subscription (item no. 4)

The author would also like to thank Stephen Green, the Curator at Lord's, and his colleagues on the Arts and Library Committee, notably Henry Wyndham, for their invaluable help and advice.

Bibliography

The principal books consulted during work on *Treasures of Lord's* were the following:

Bailey, Philip; Thorn, Philip; and Wynne-Thomas, Peter, *Who's Who of Cricketers* (Newnes Books with the Association of Cricket Statisticians, 1984)

Frith, David, *Pageant of Cricket* (Macmillan, 1987)

Harris, Lord and Ashley-Cooper, F. S., *Lord's and the MCC* (Herbert Jenkins, 1920)

Lewis, Tony, *Double Century* (Hodder and Stoughton, 1987)

Moorhouse, Geoffrey, *Lord's* (Hodder and Stoughton, 1983)

Simon, Robin and Smart, Alastair, *John Player Art of Cricket* (John Player, 1983)

Swanton, E. W., *Barclays World of Cricket* (Collins Willow 1980 and 1986)

Warner, P. F., *Imperial Cricket* (London and Counties Press Association, 1912)

And of course many editions of *Wisden's Cricketers' Almanack* and *Who's Who*

Index